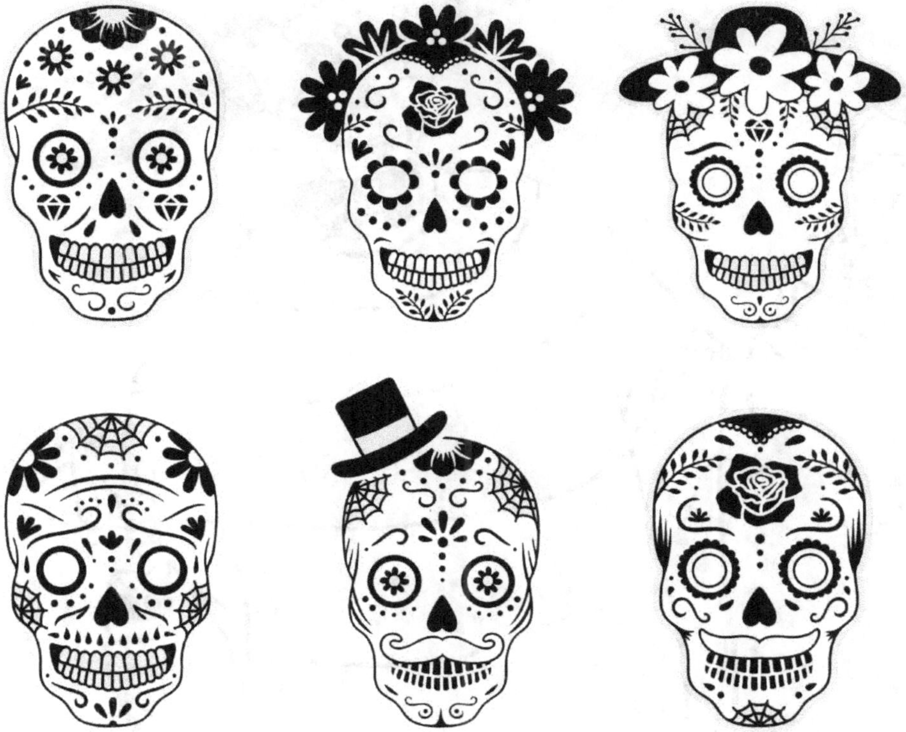

This Coloring Book belongs to

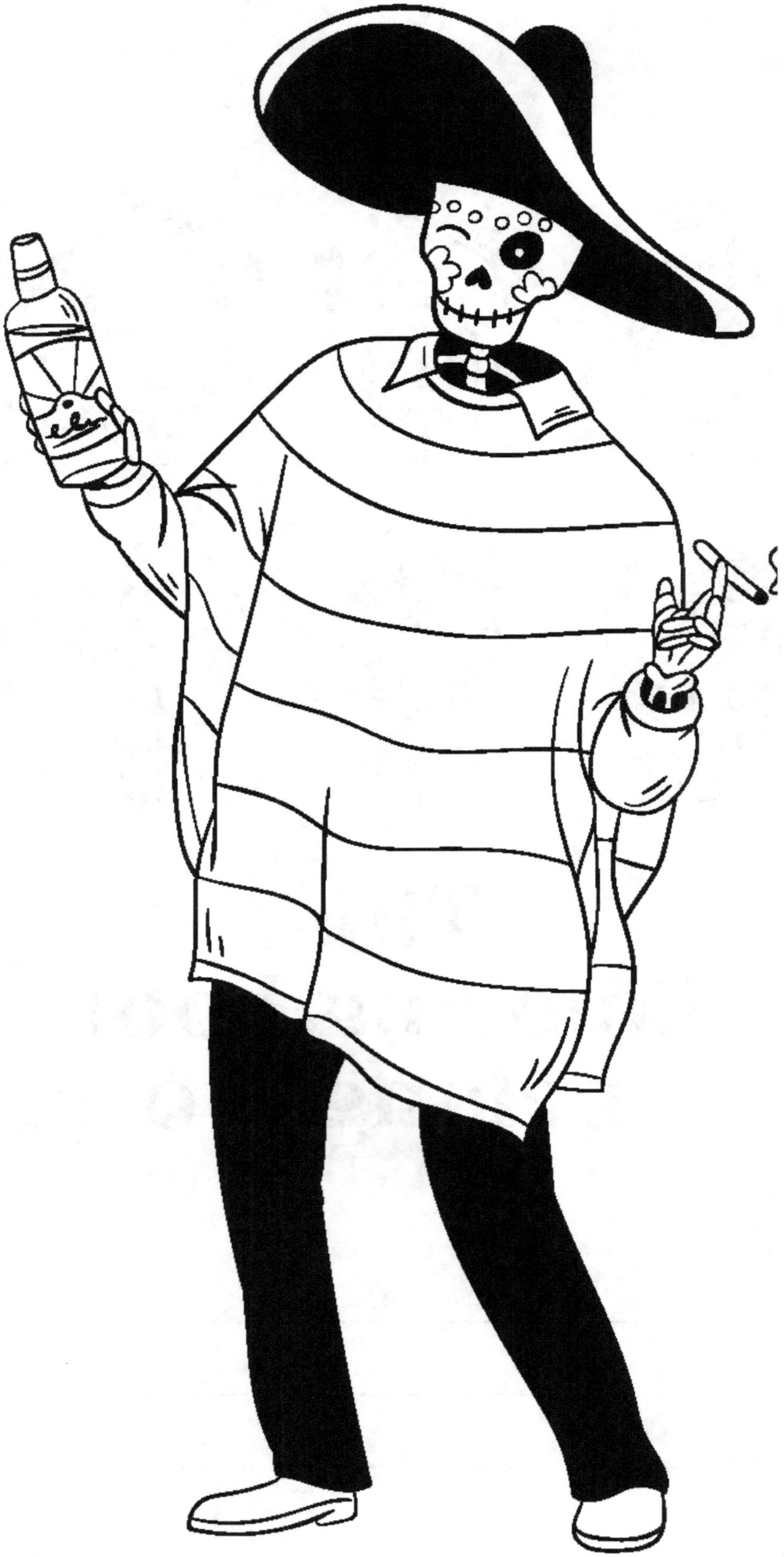

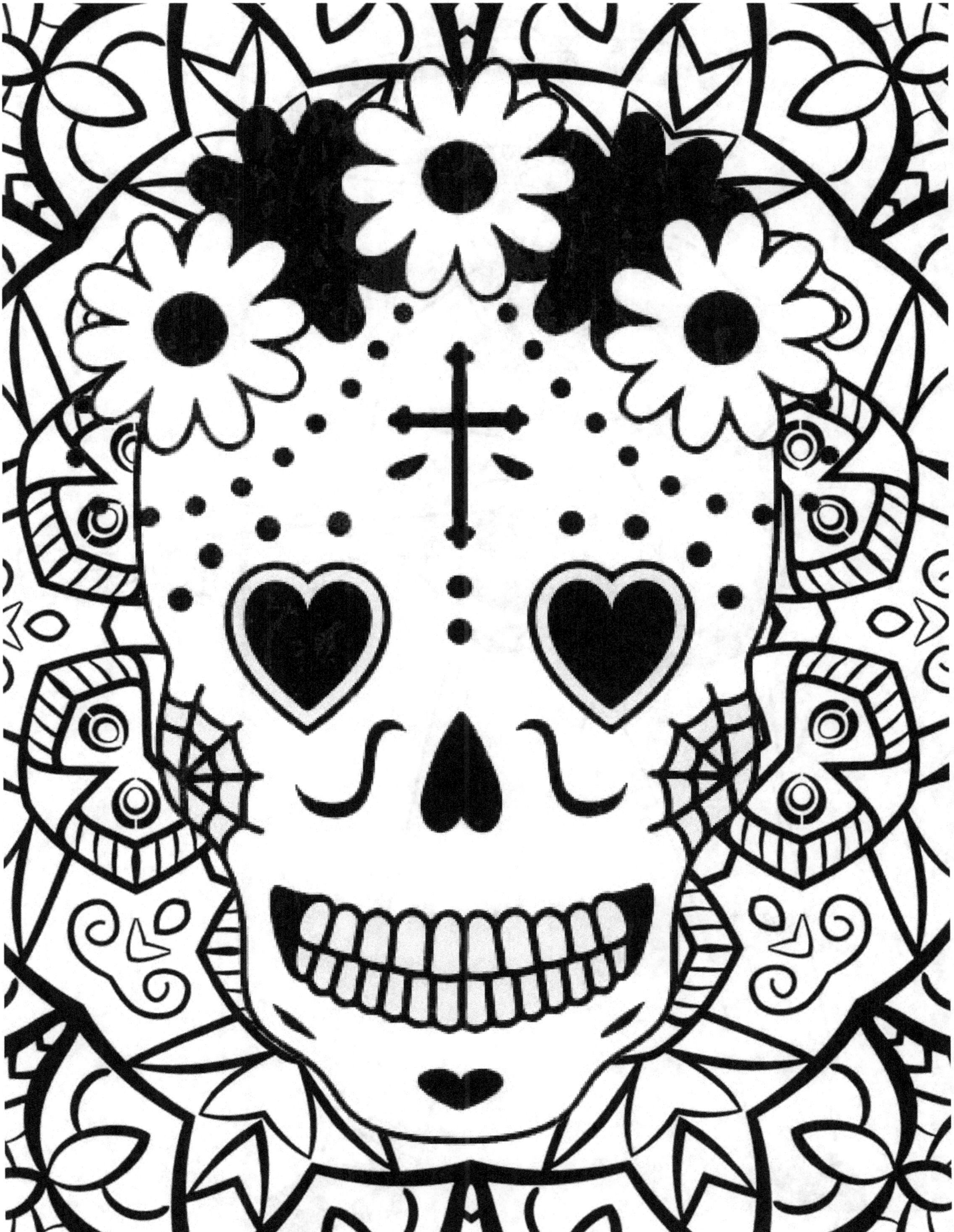

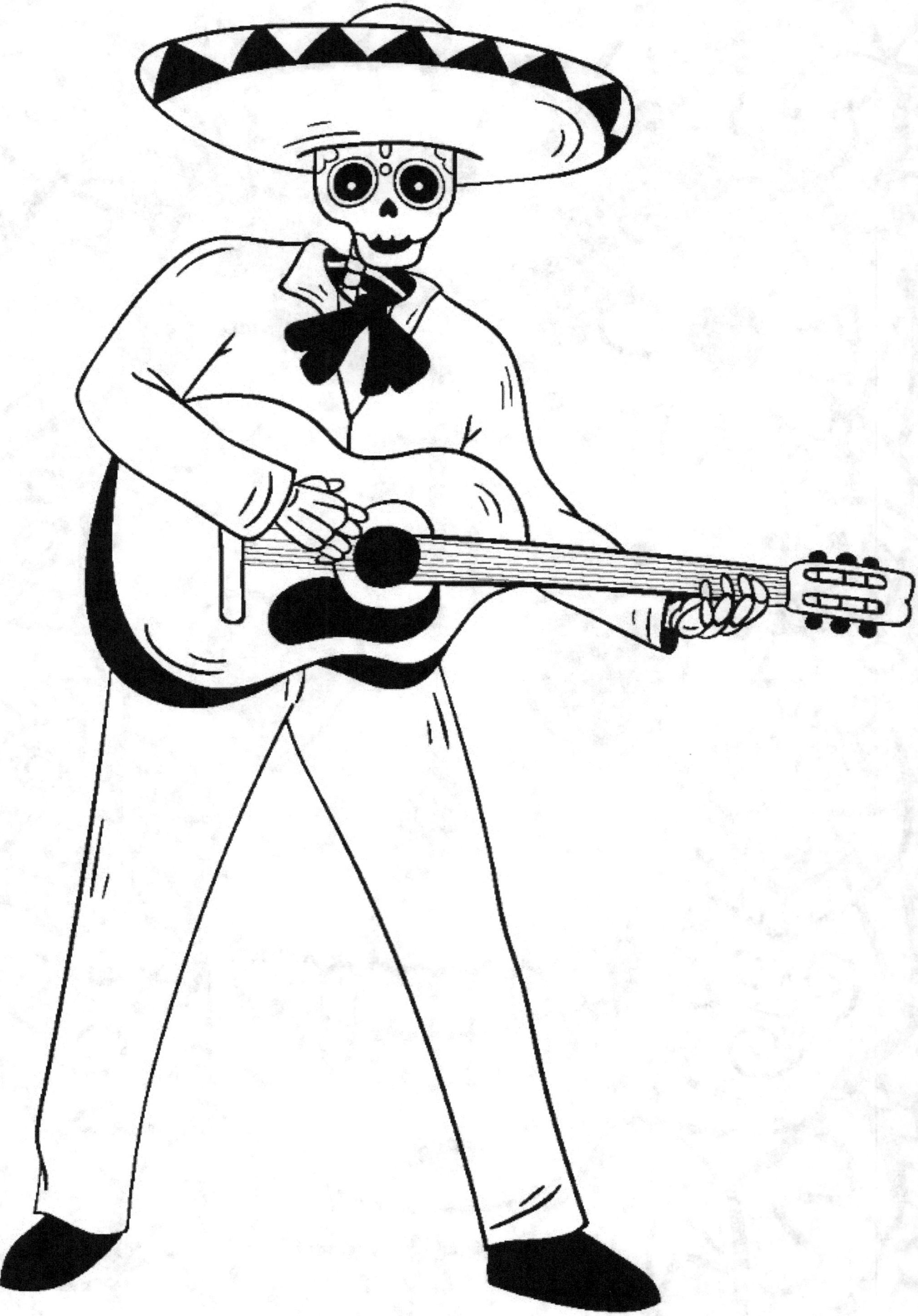

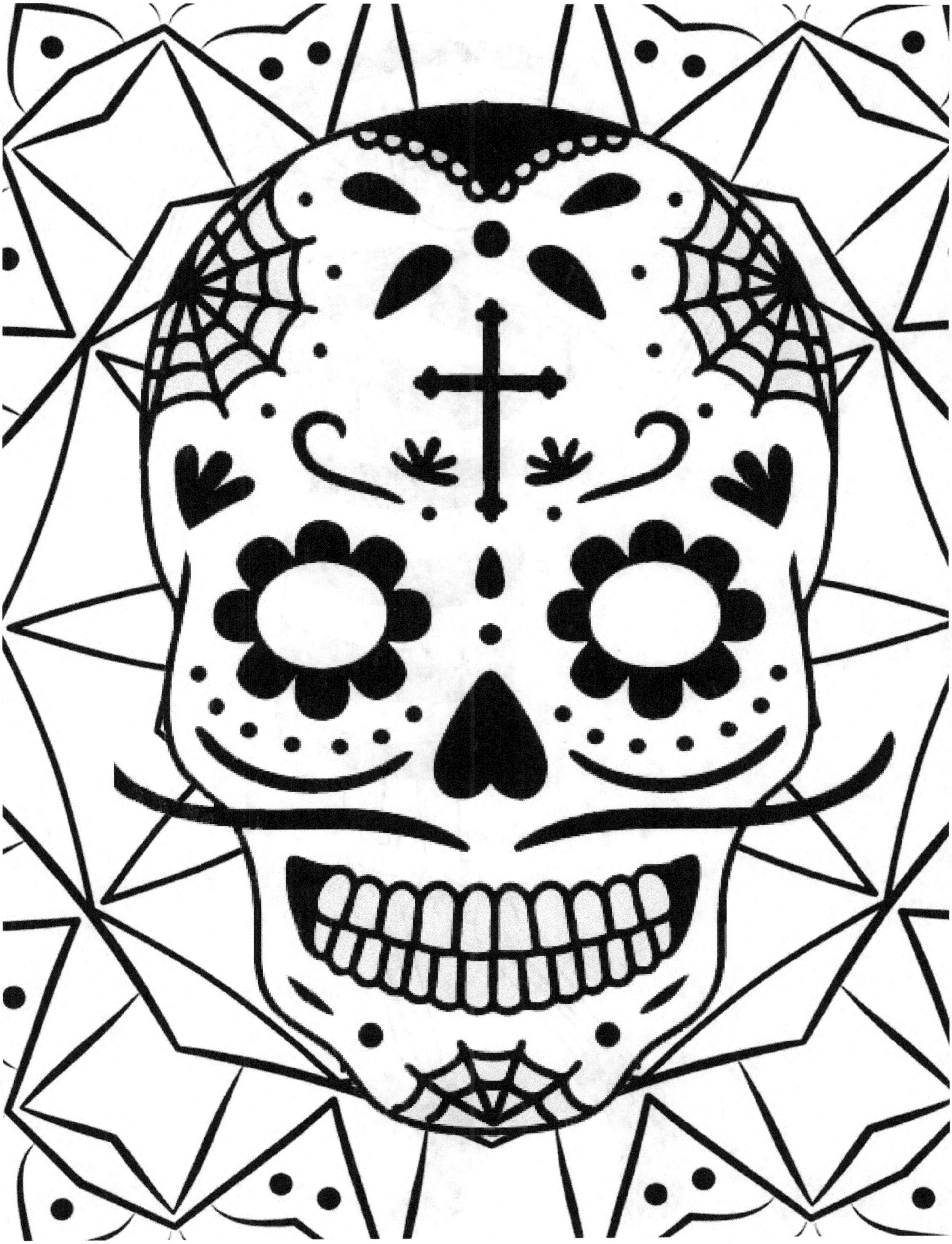

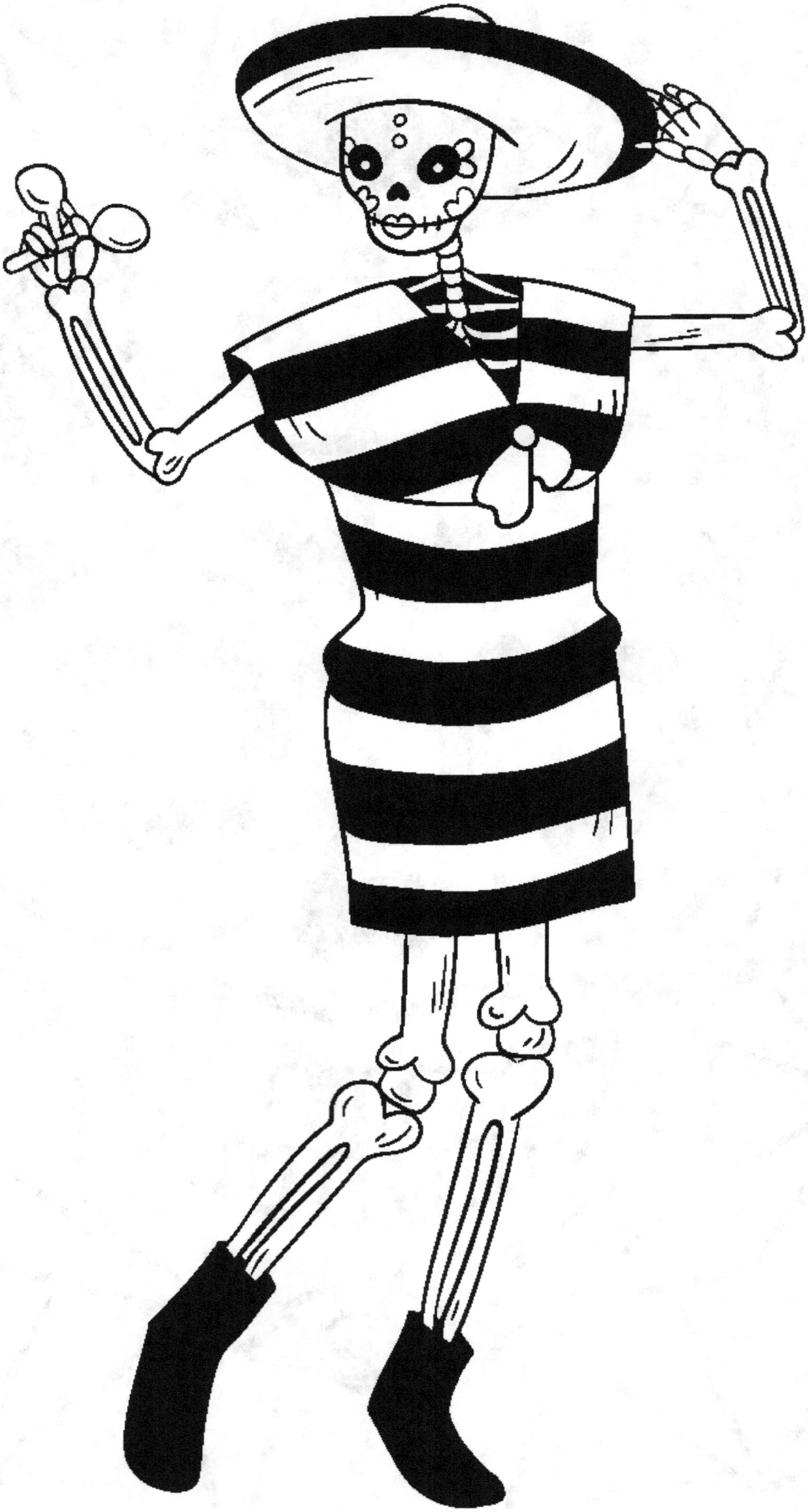

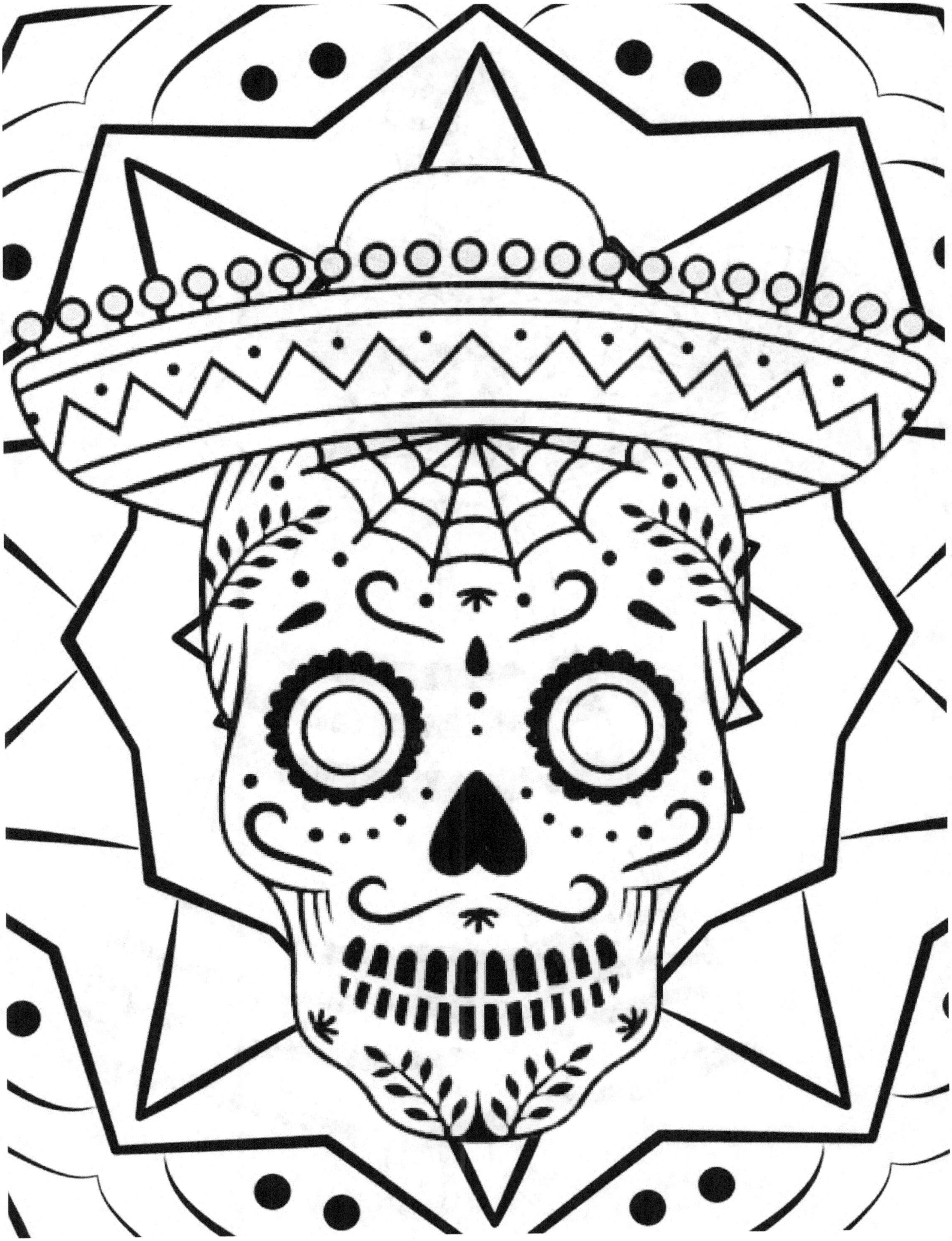

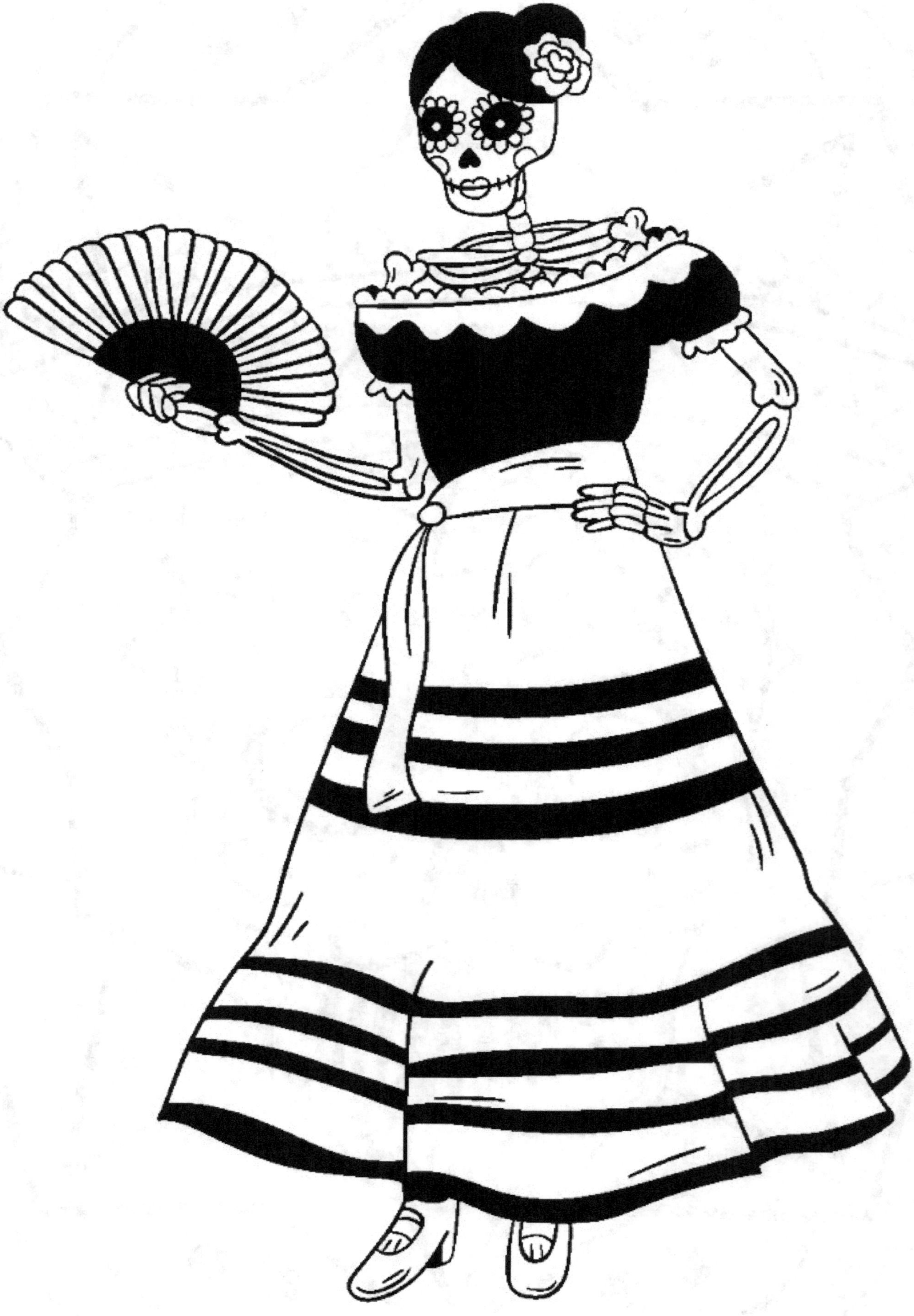

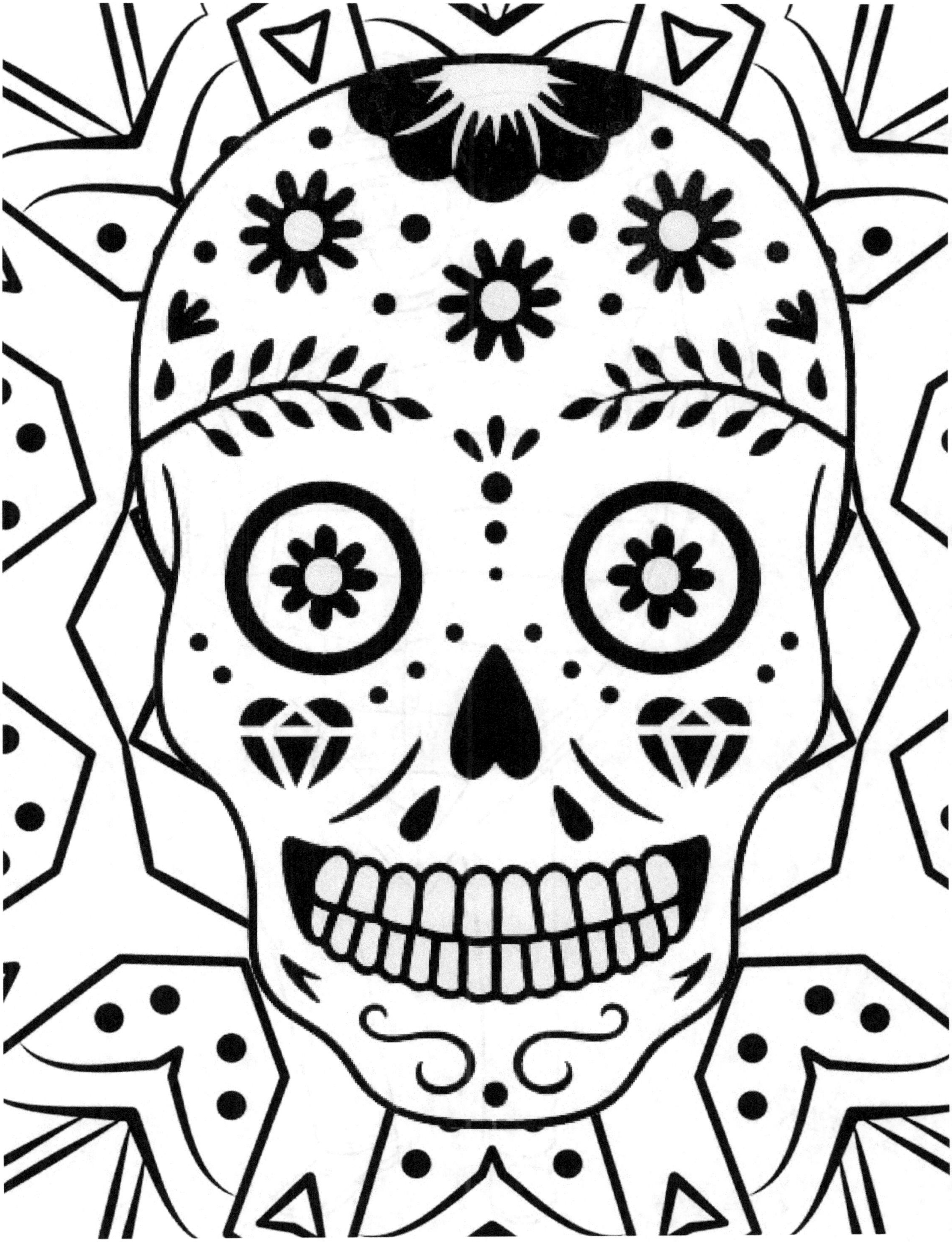

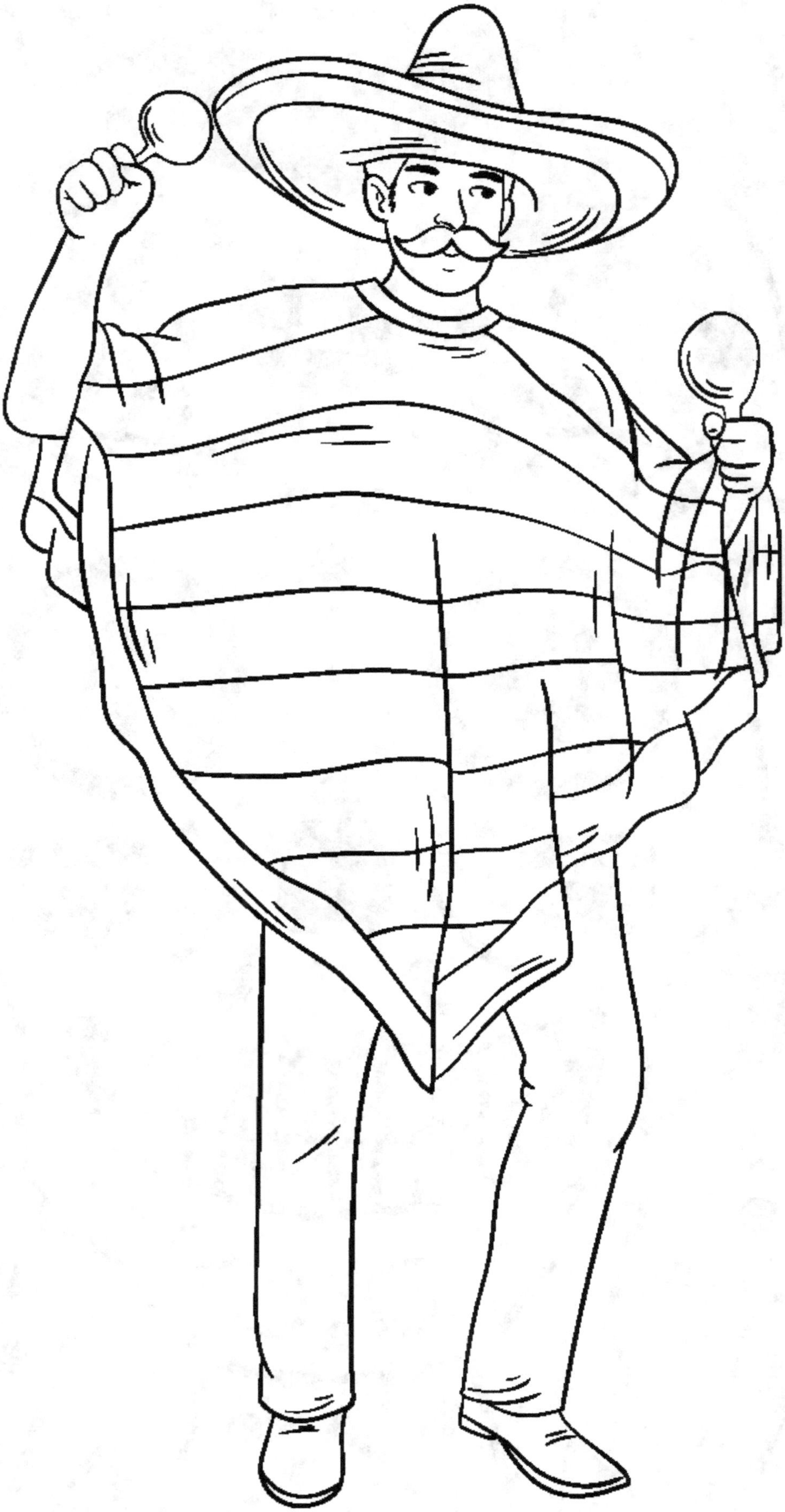

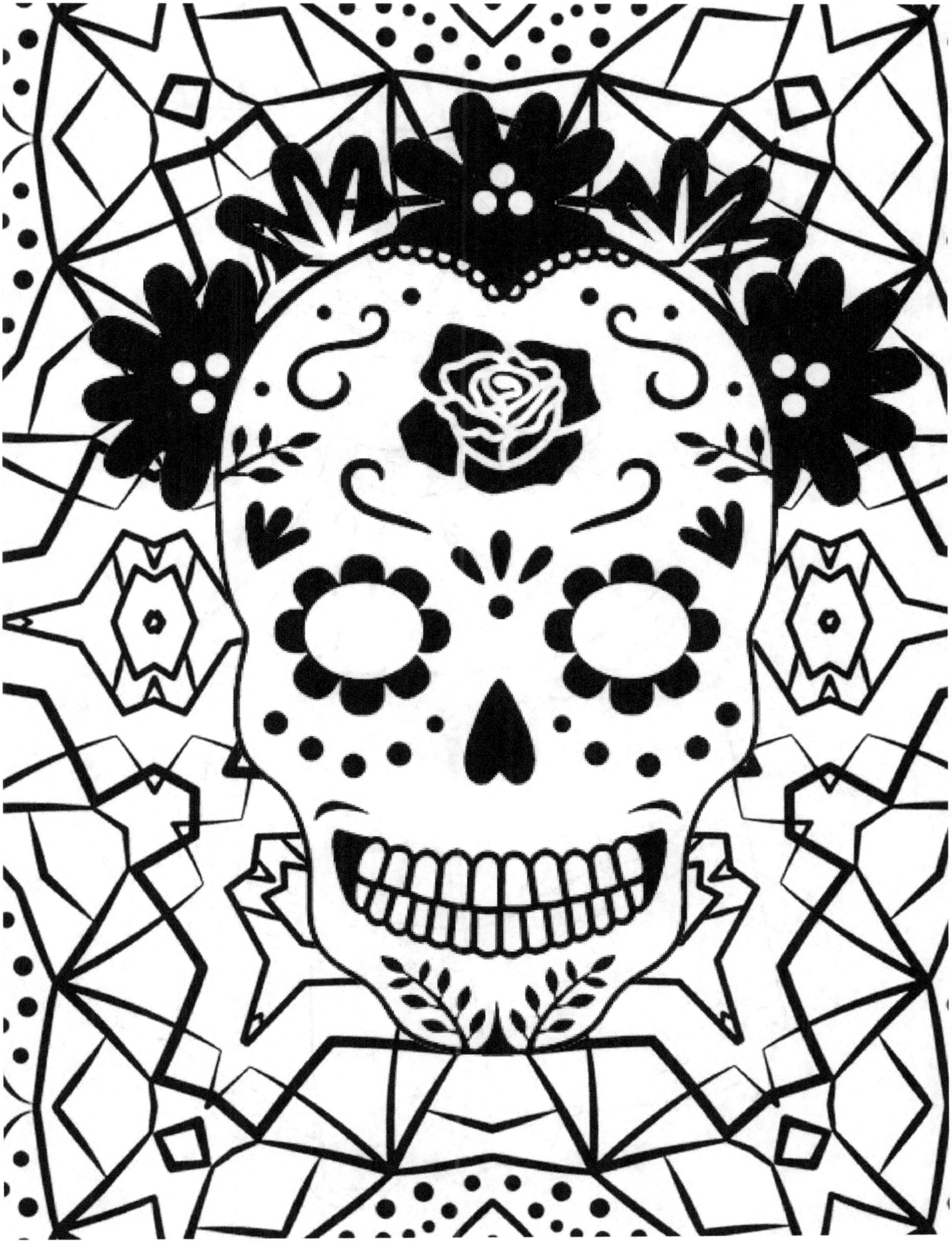

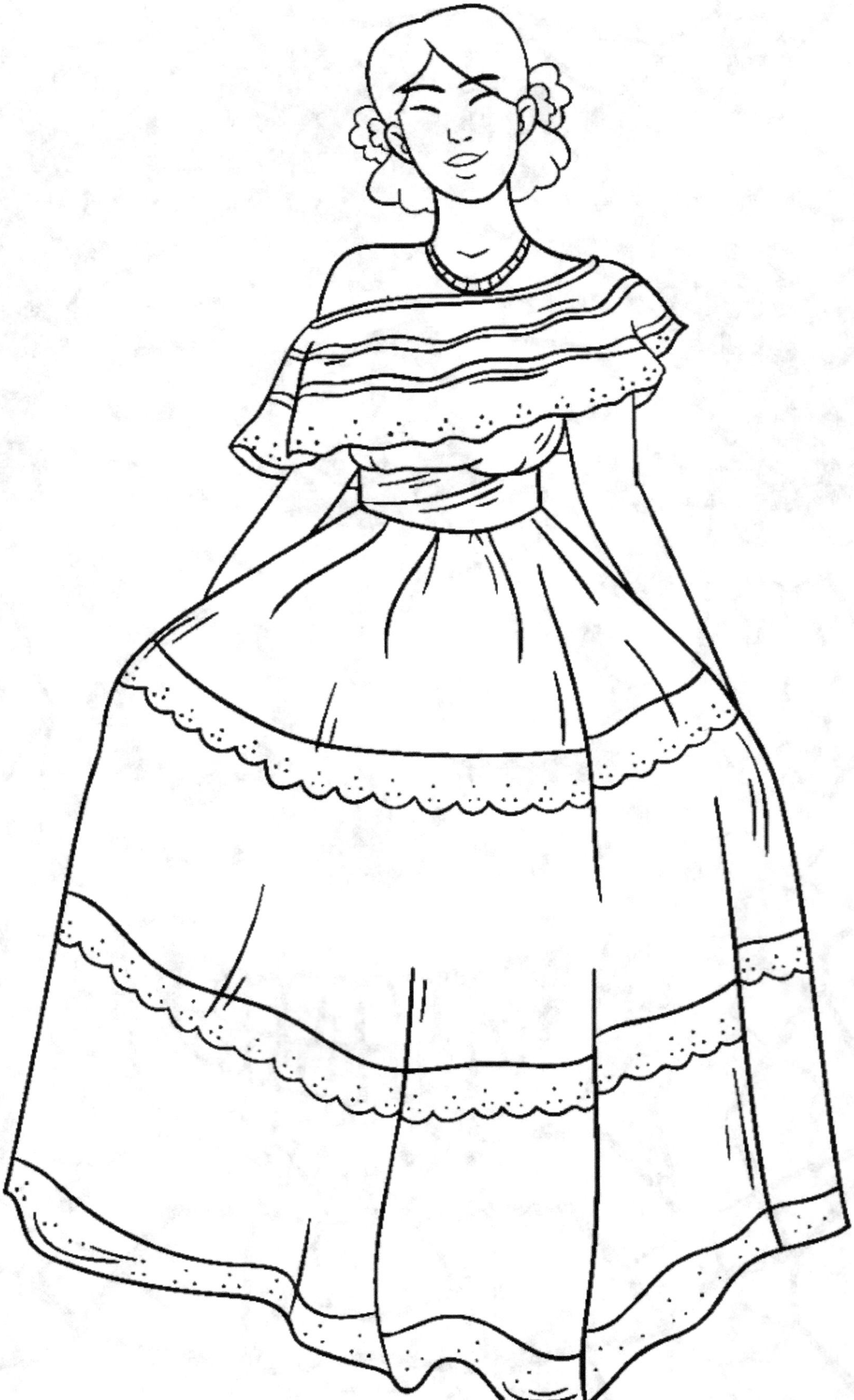

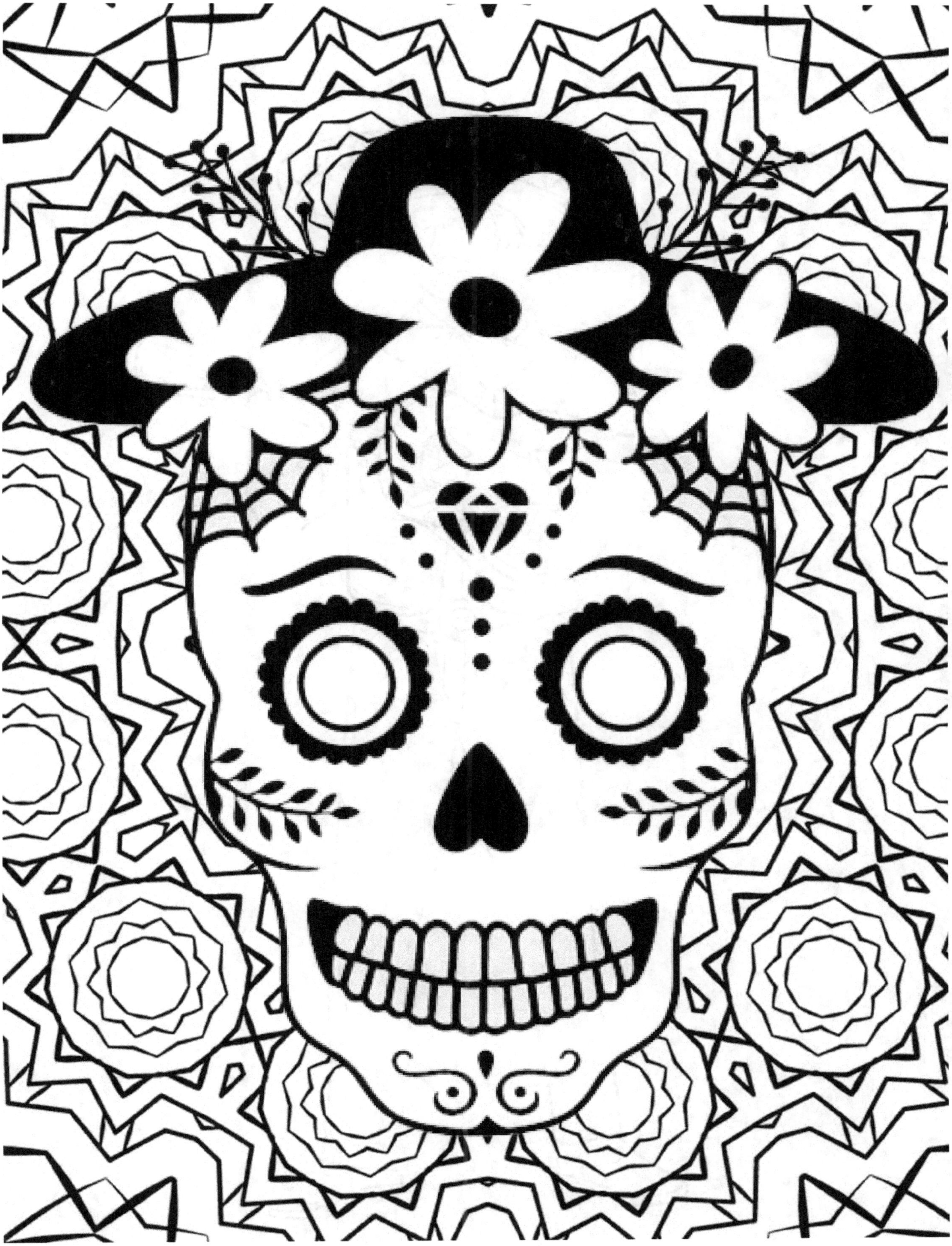

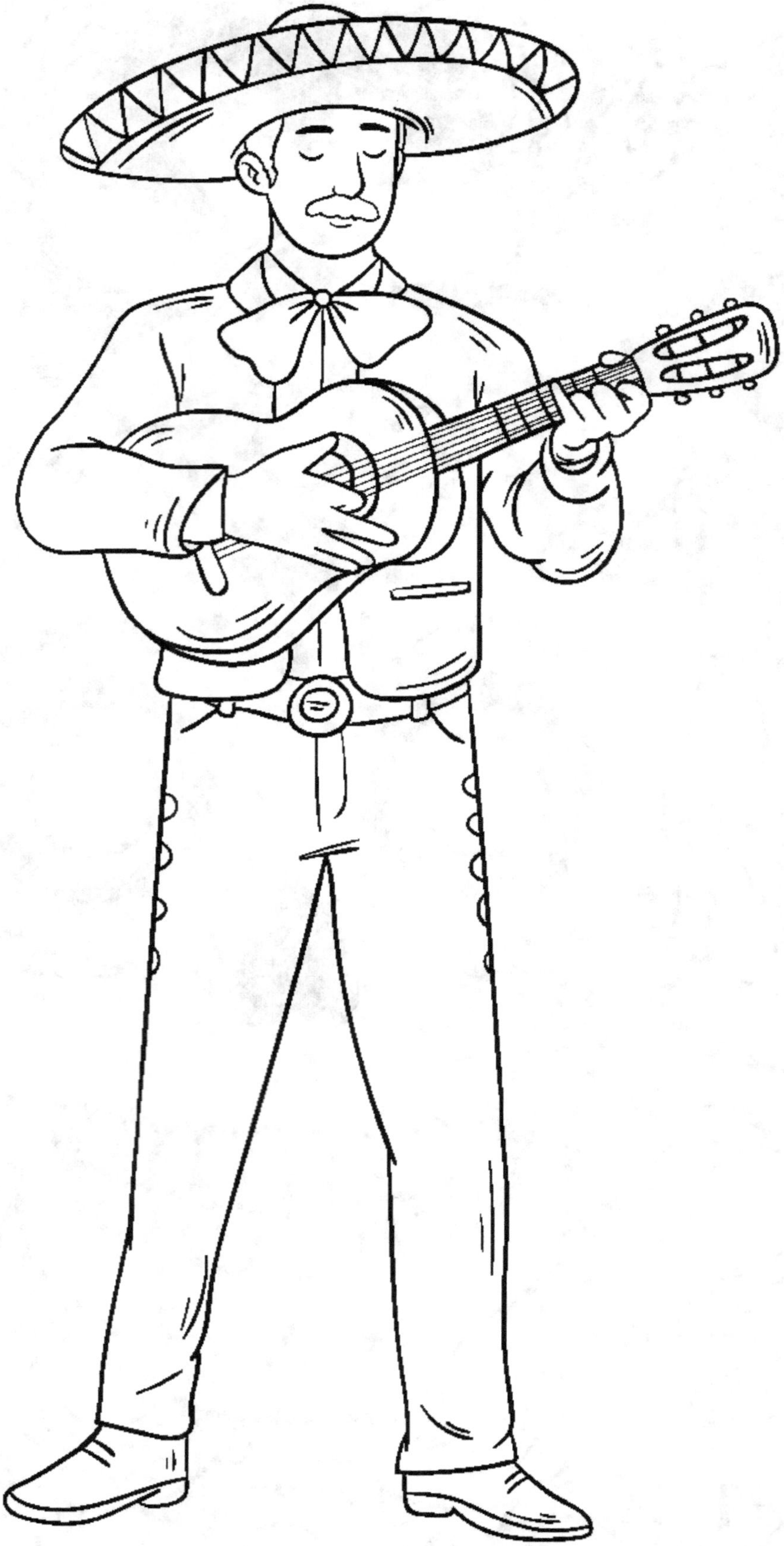

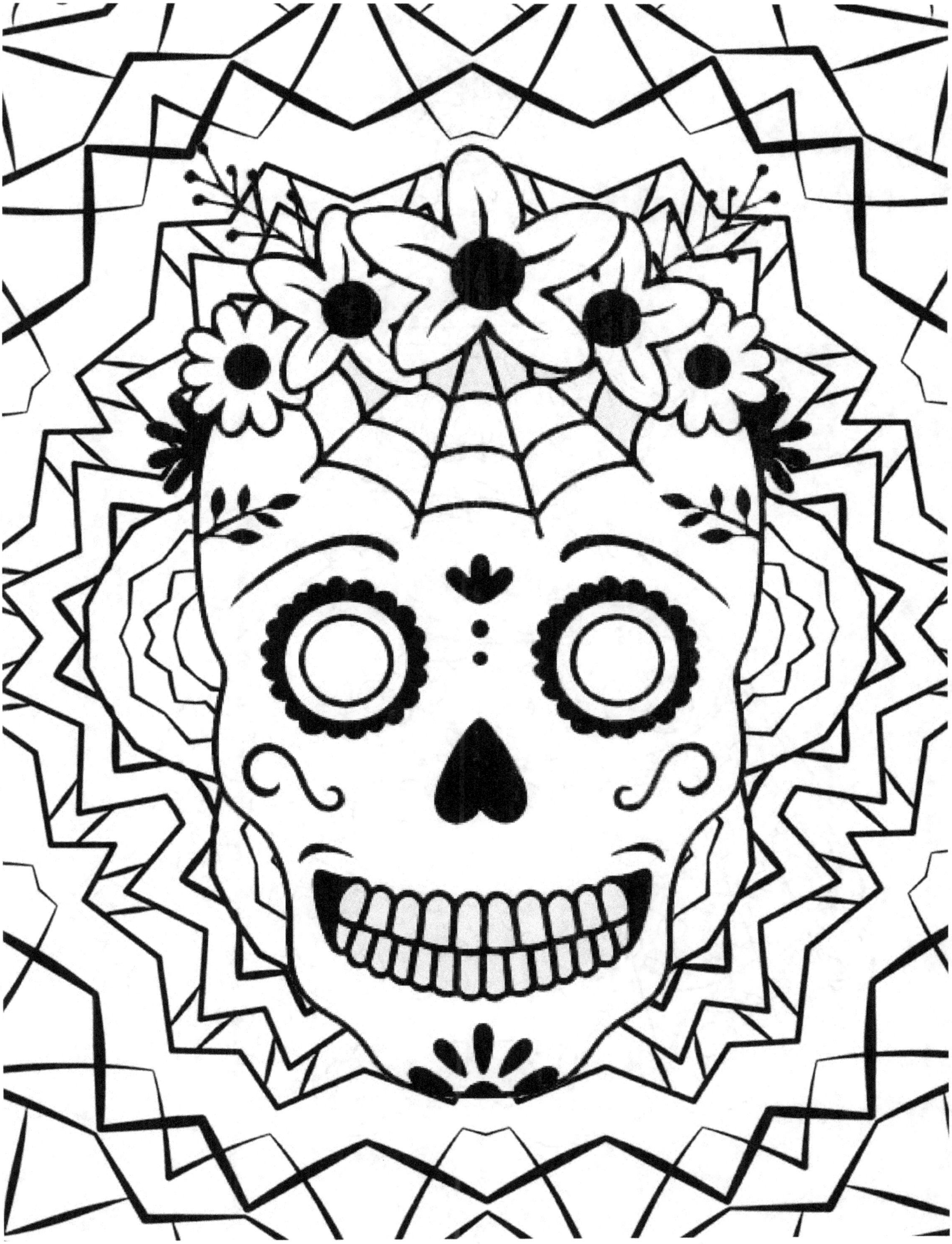

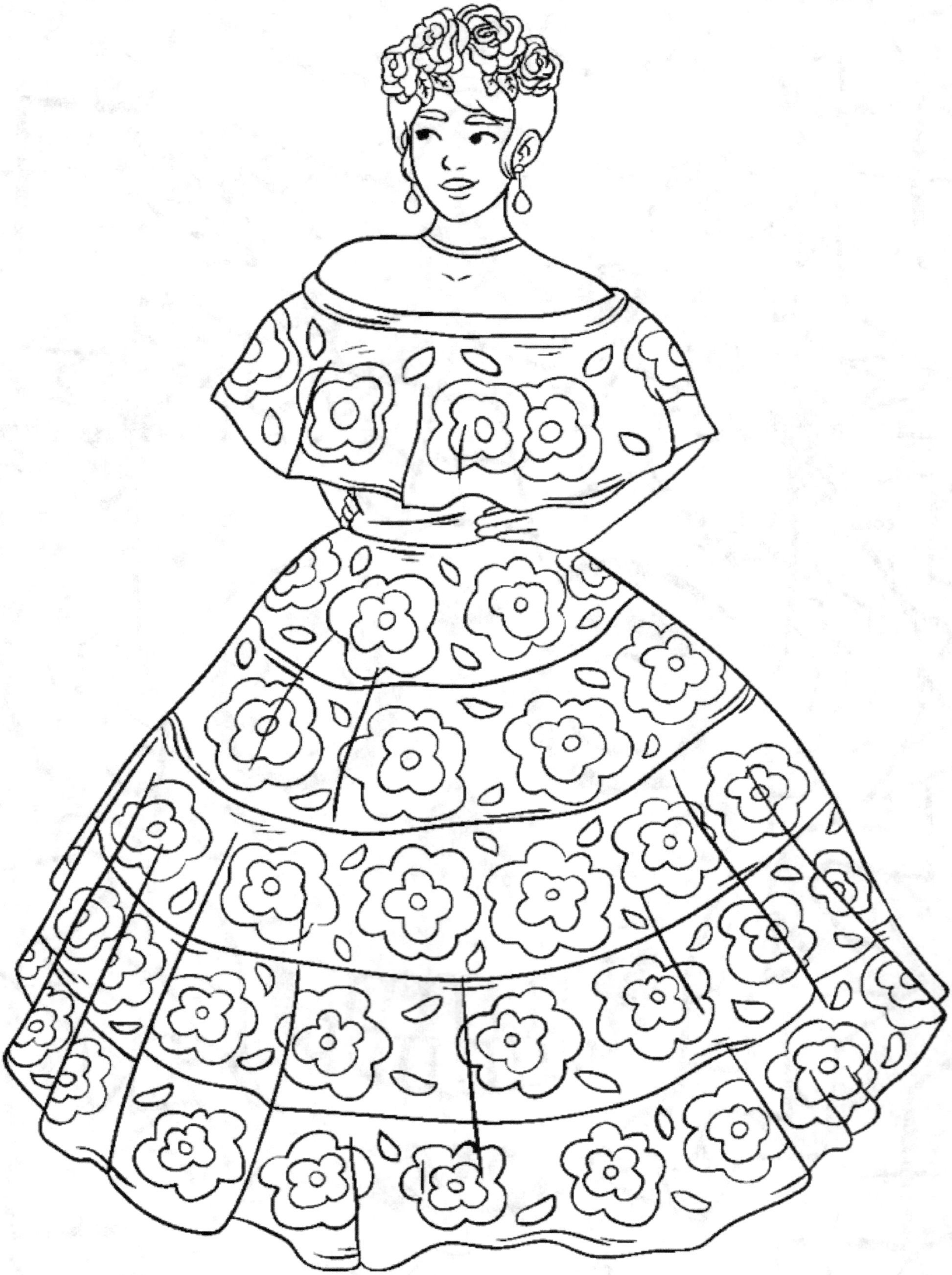

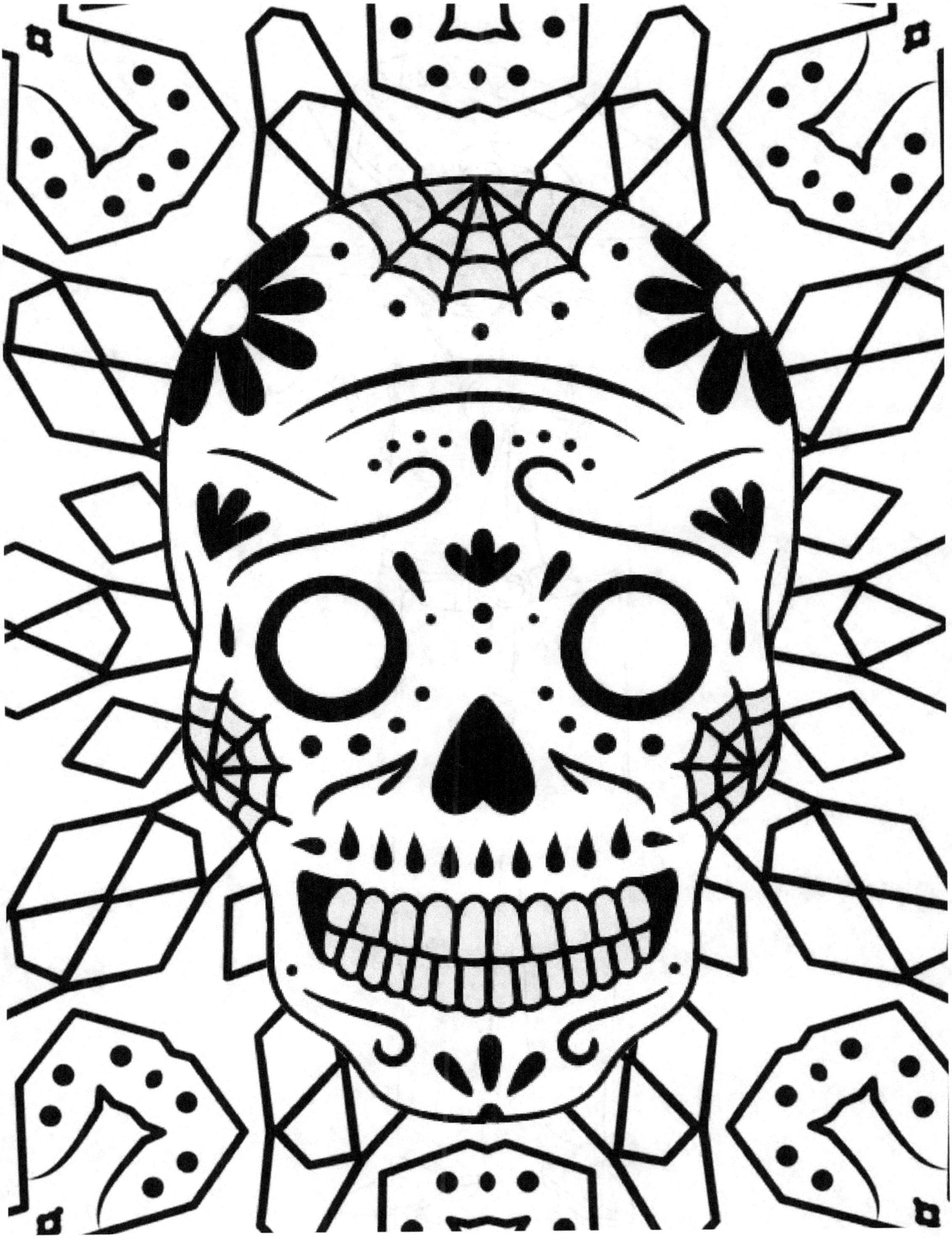

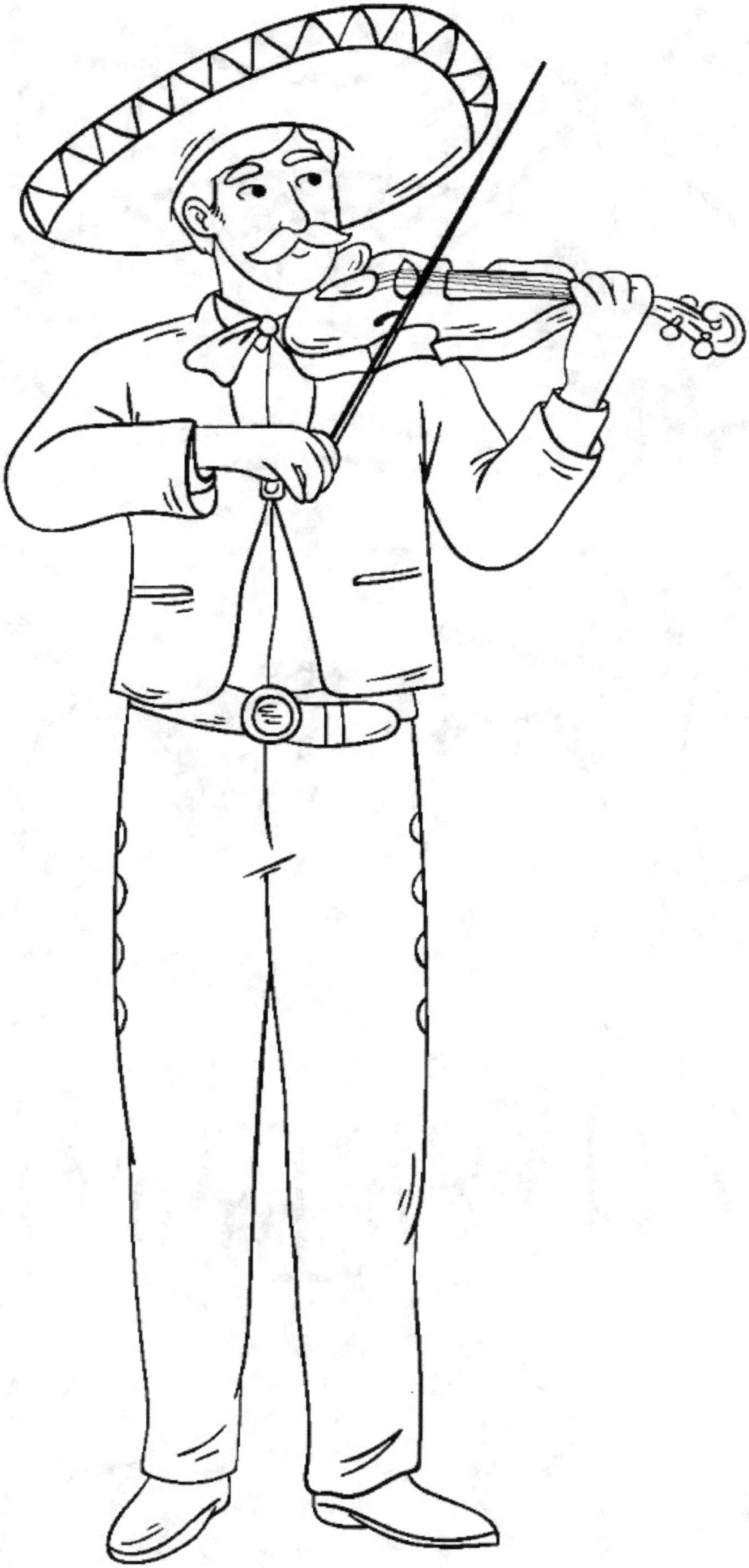

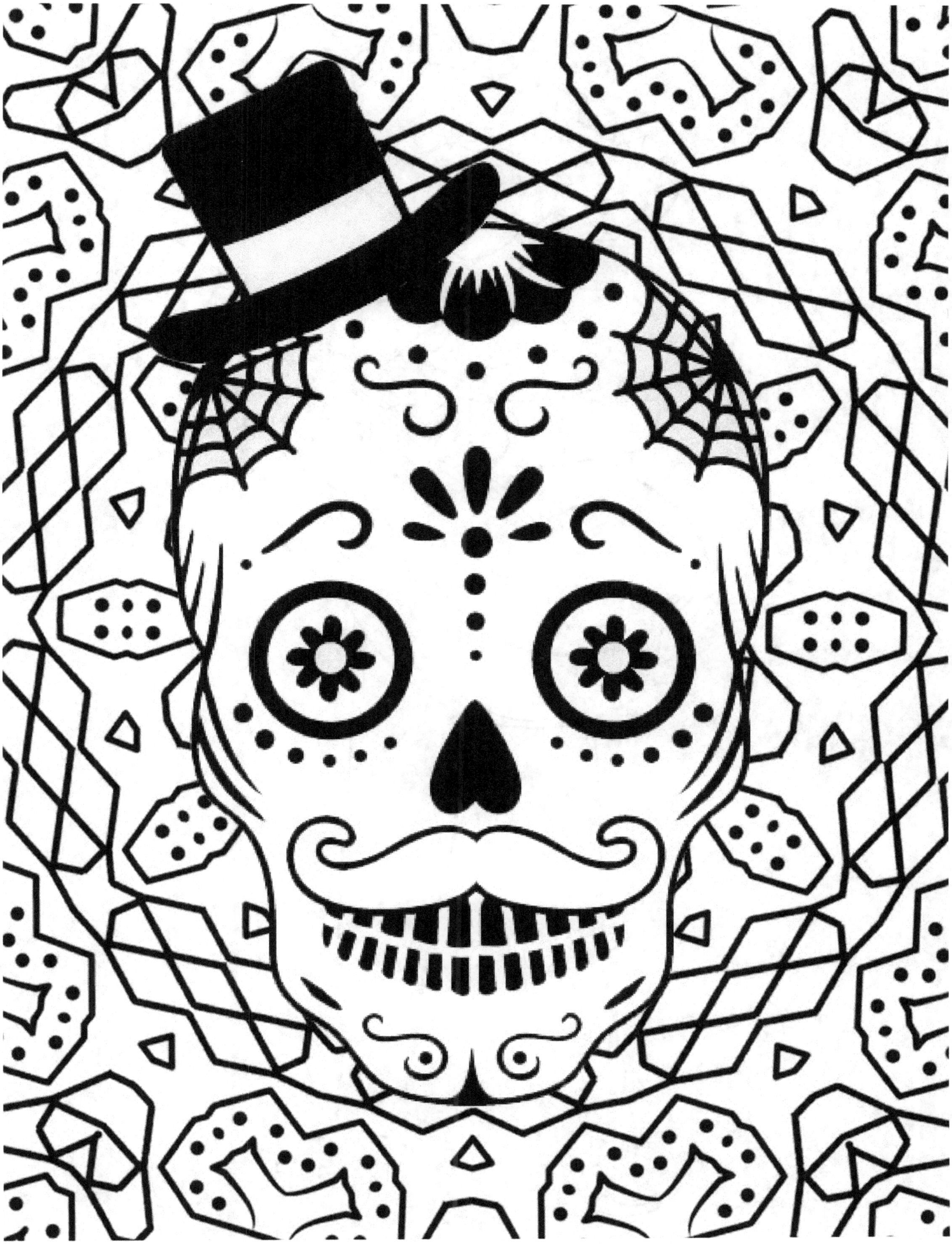

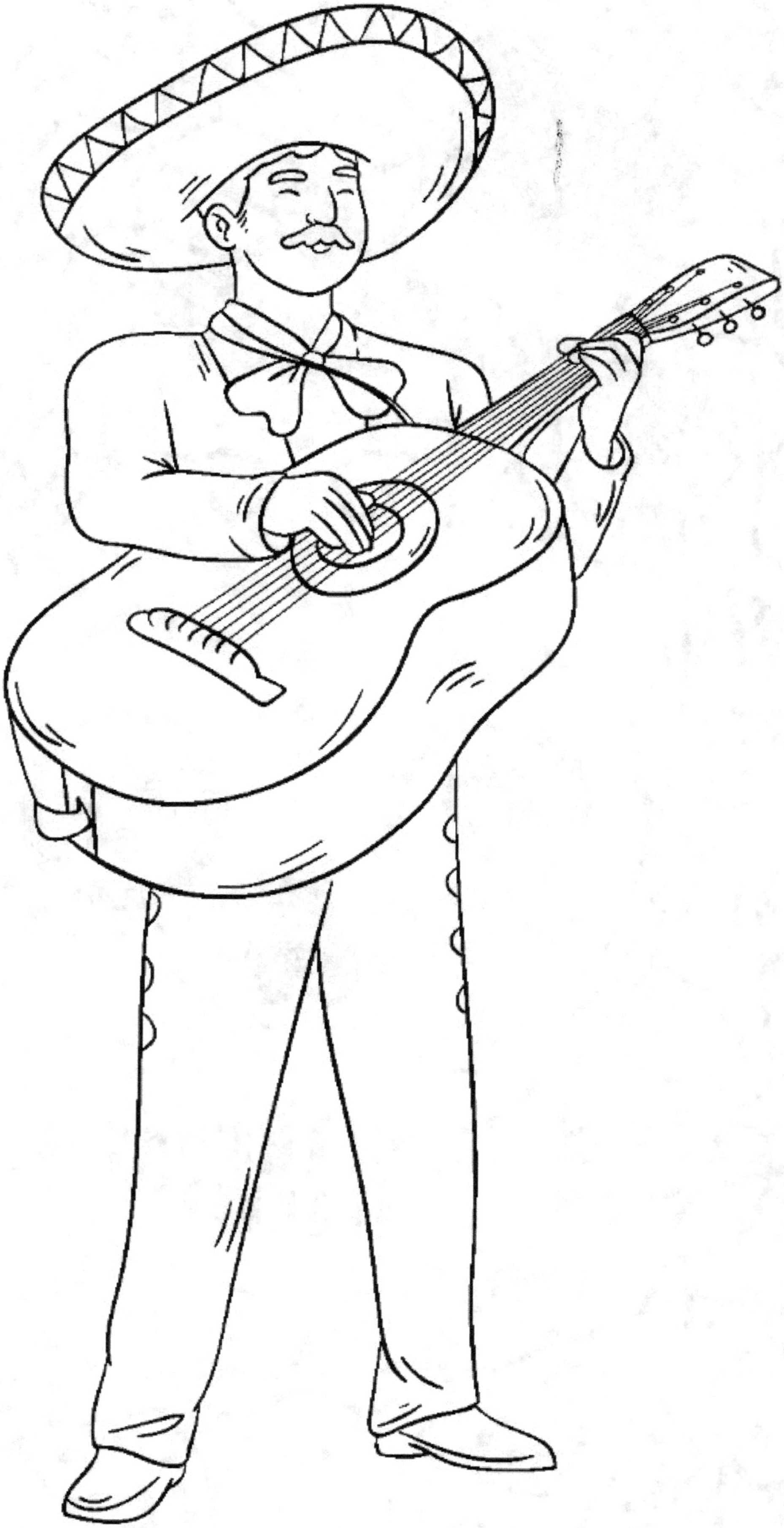

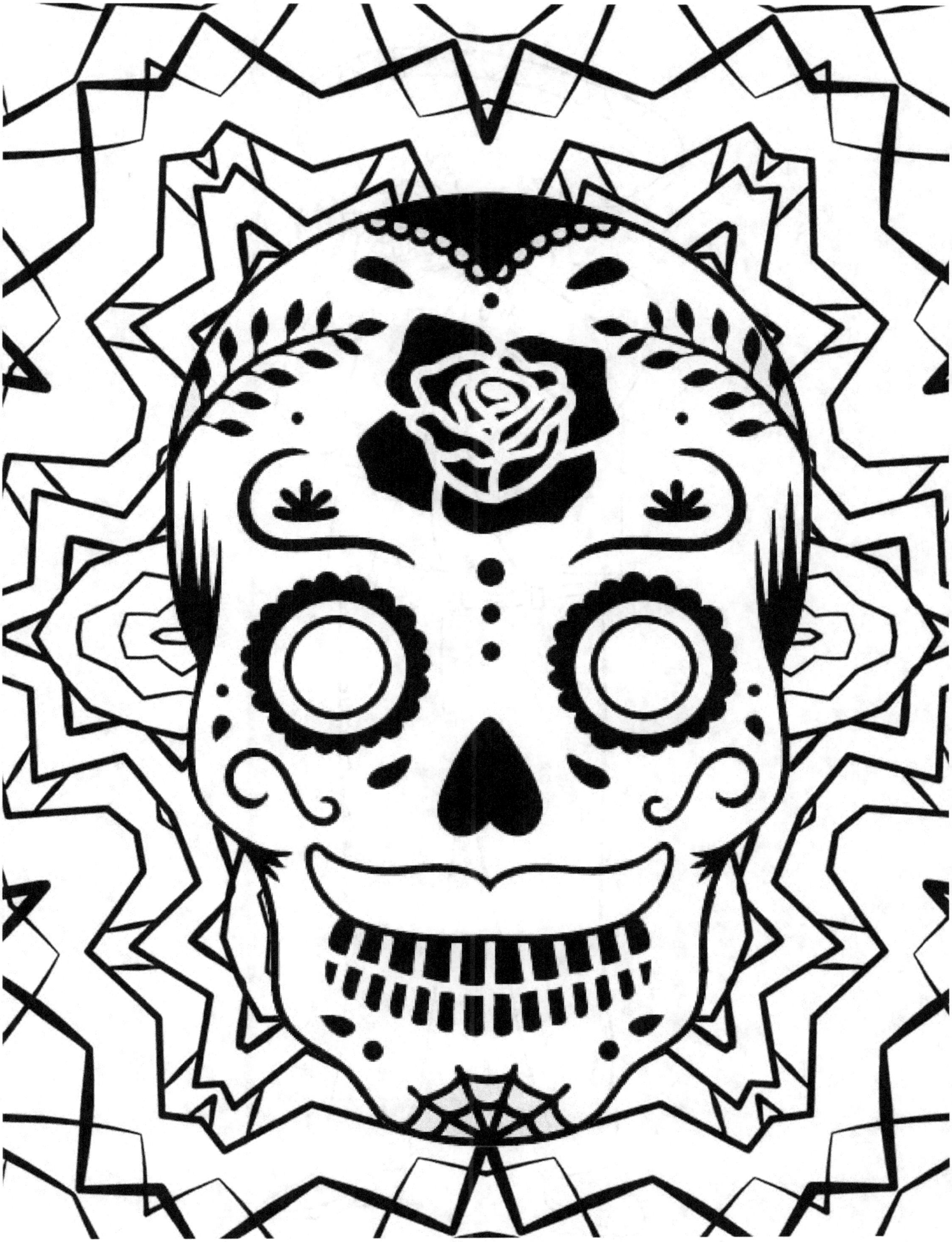

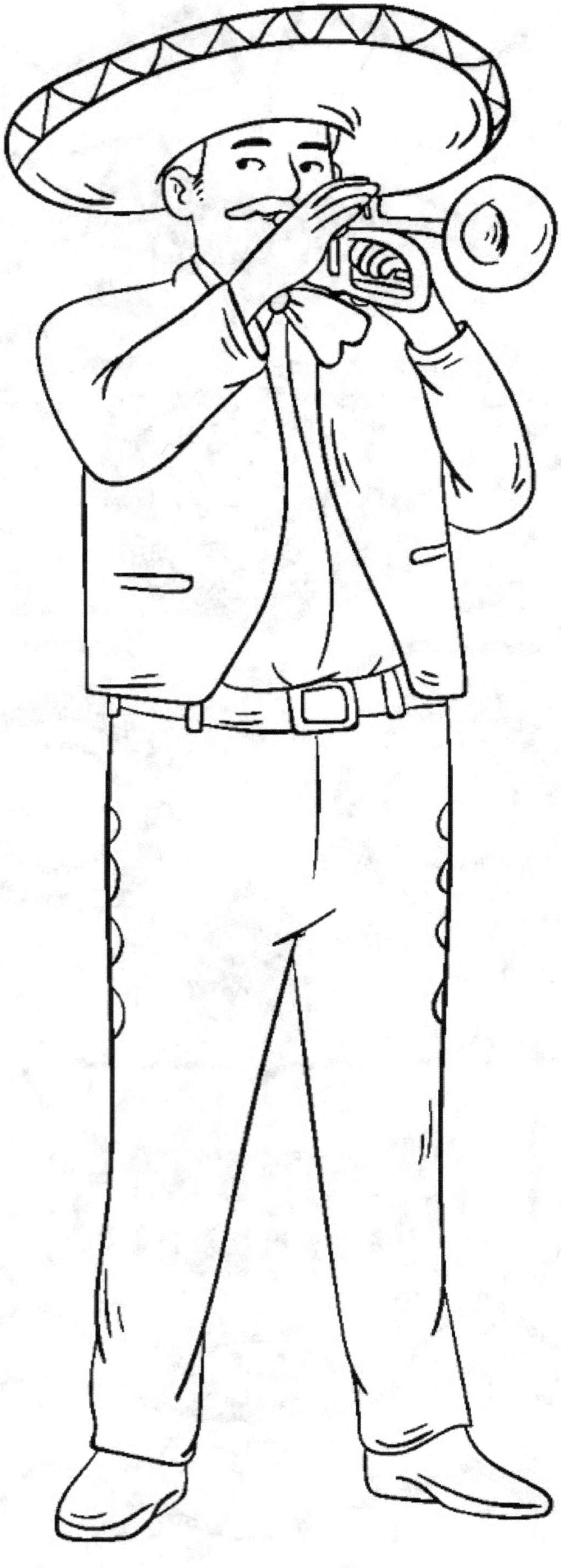

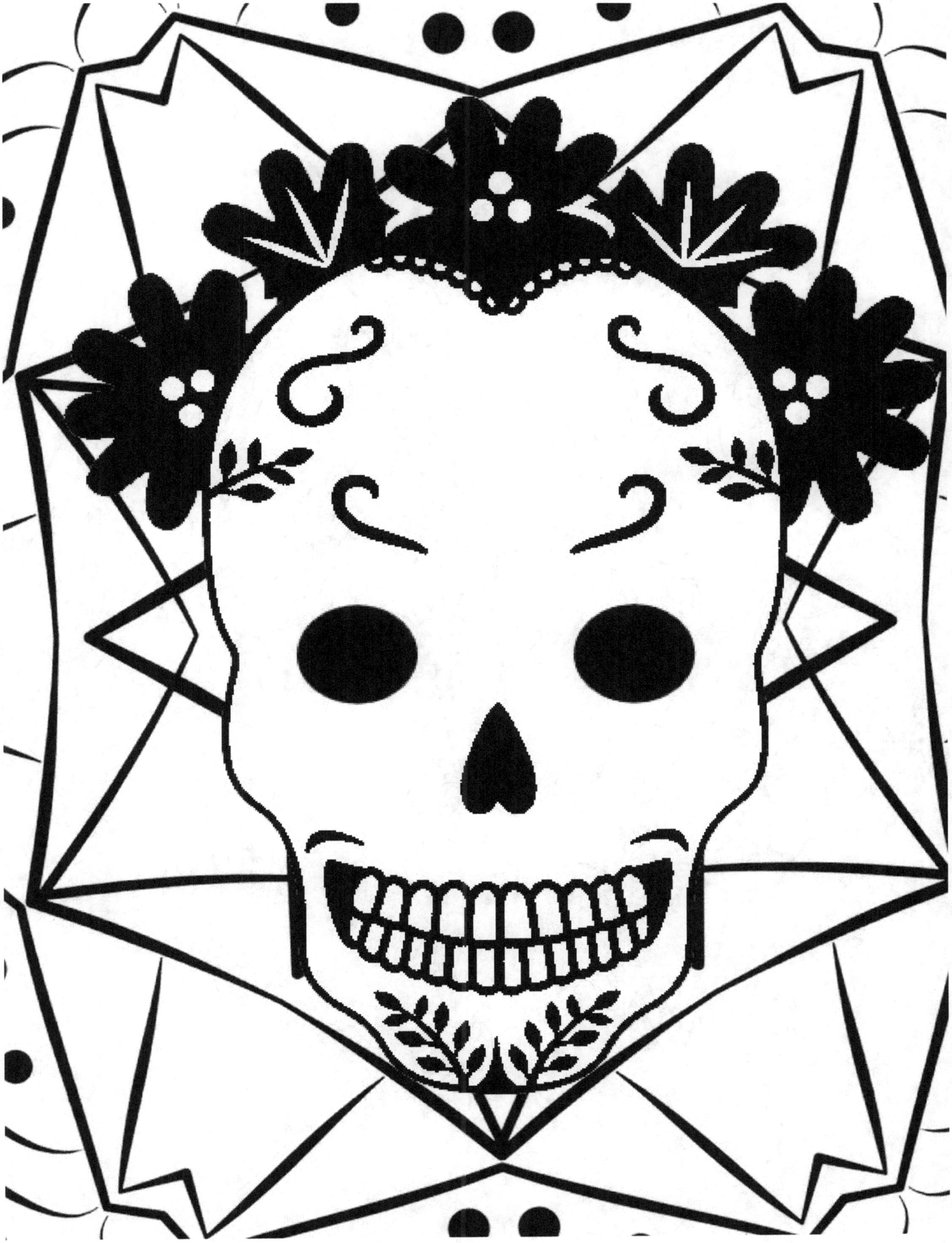

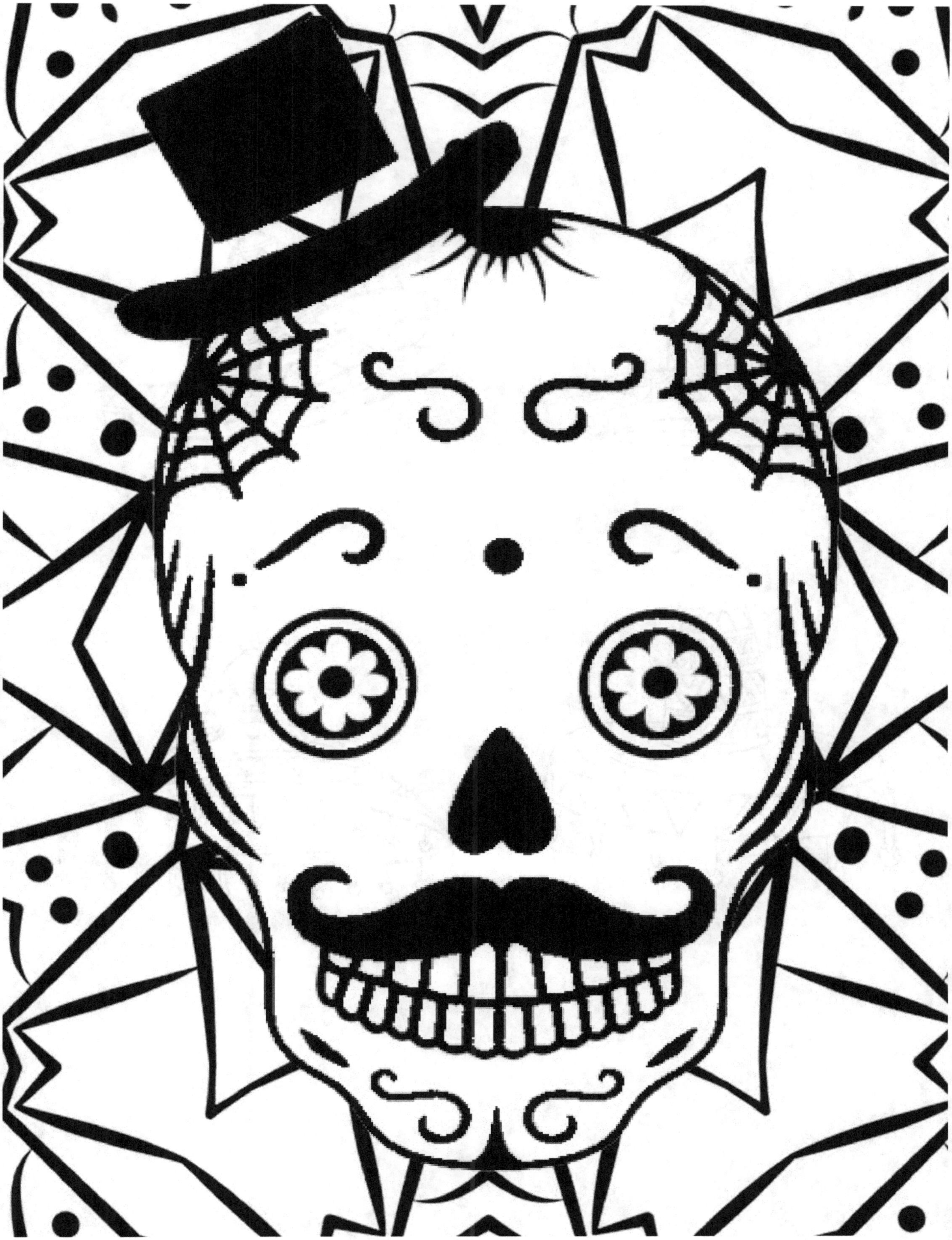

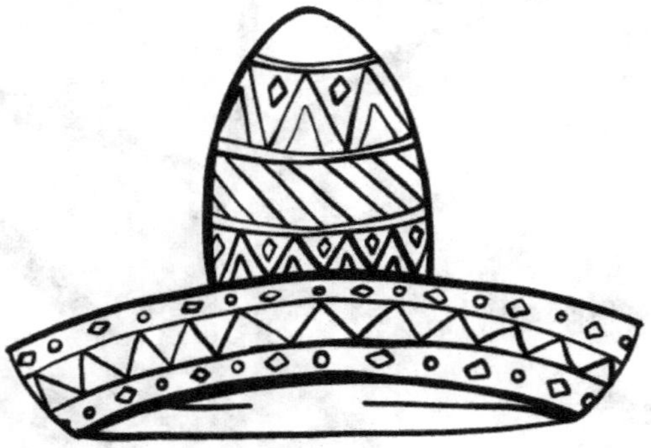
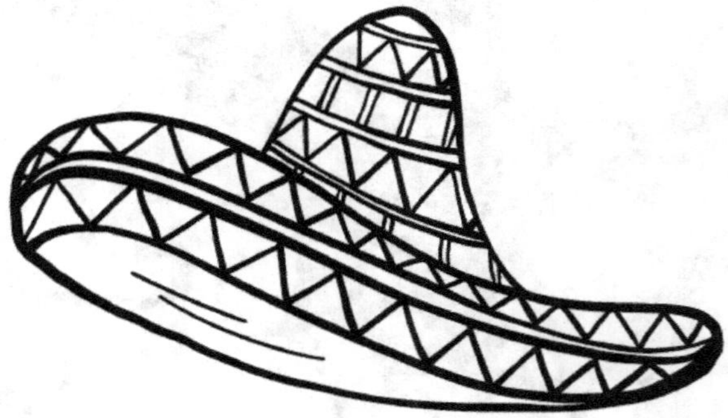
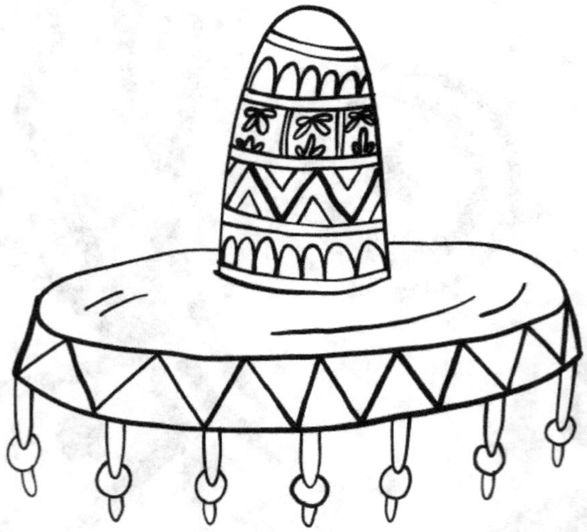
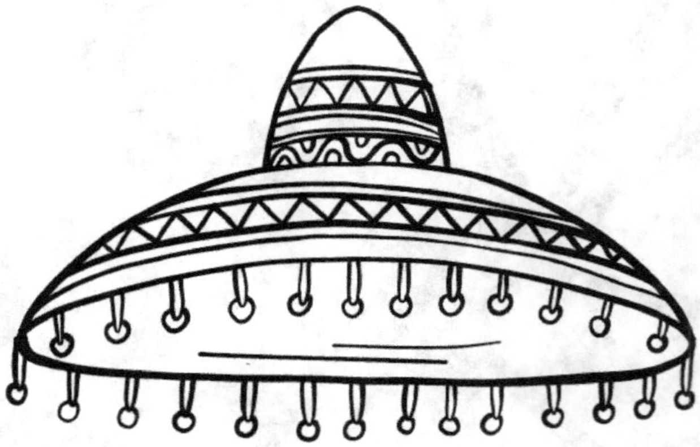

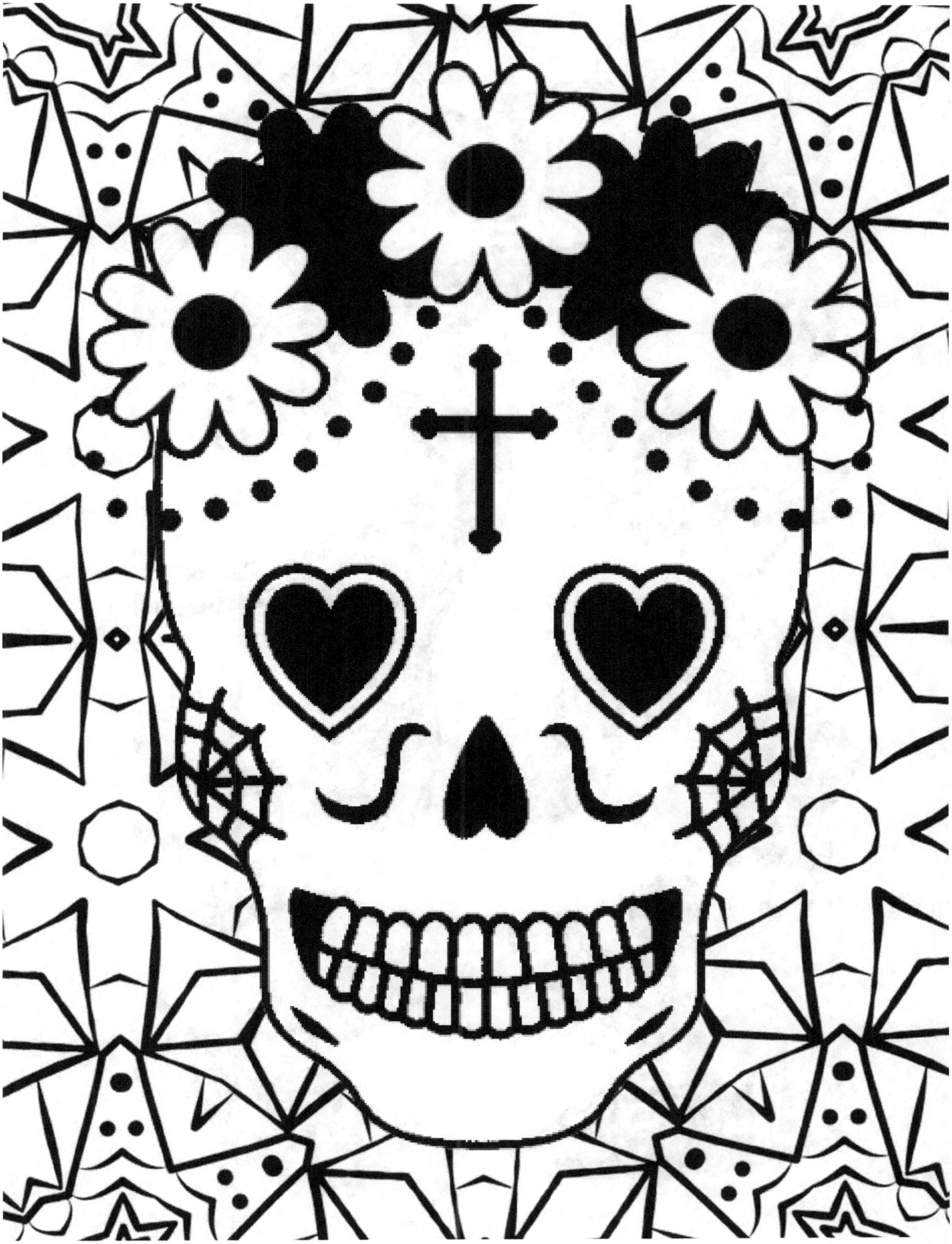

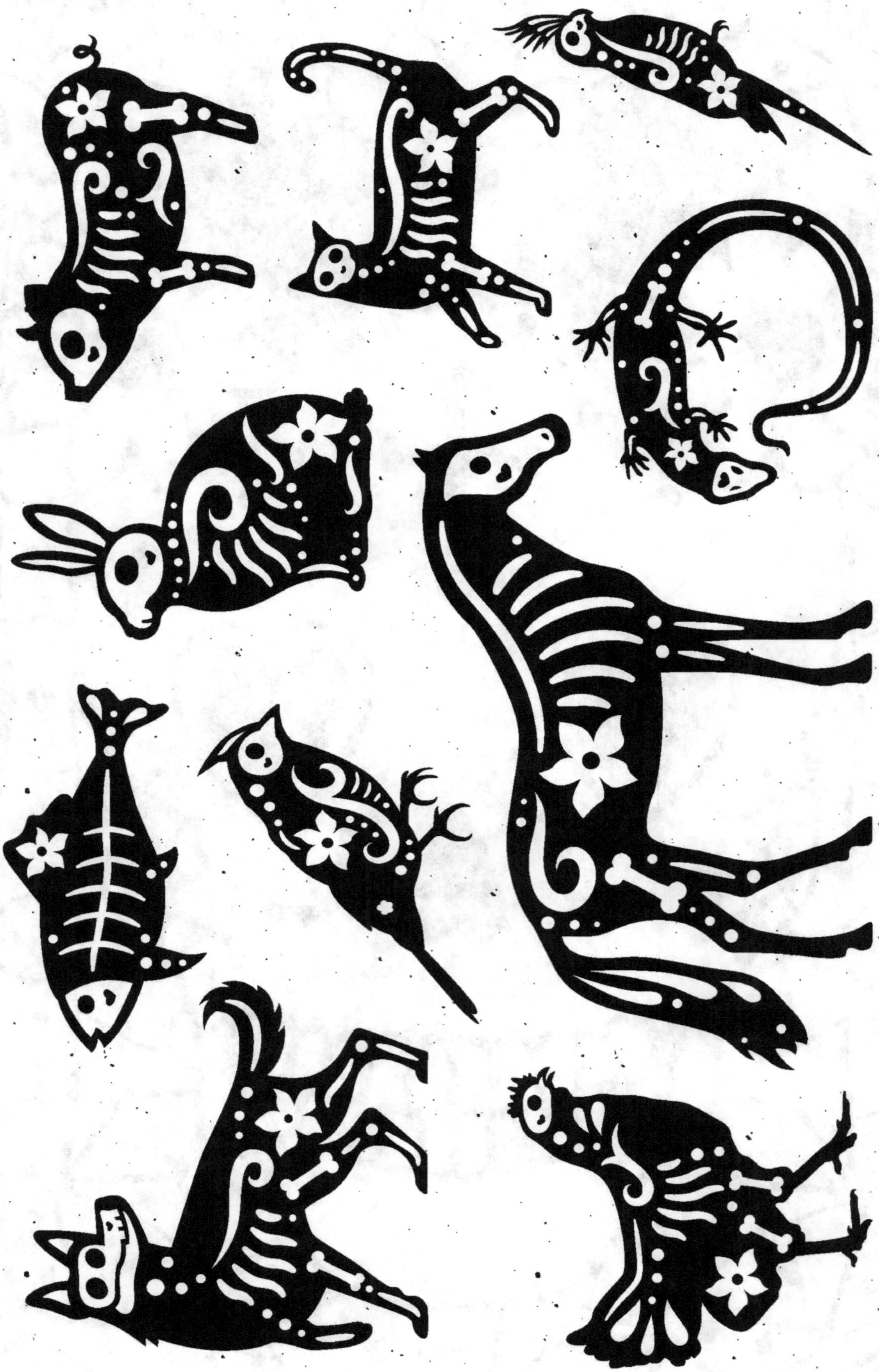

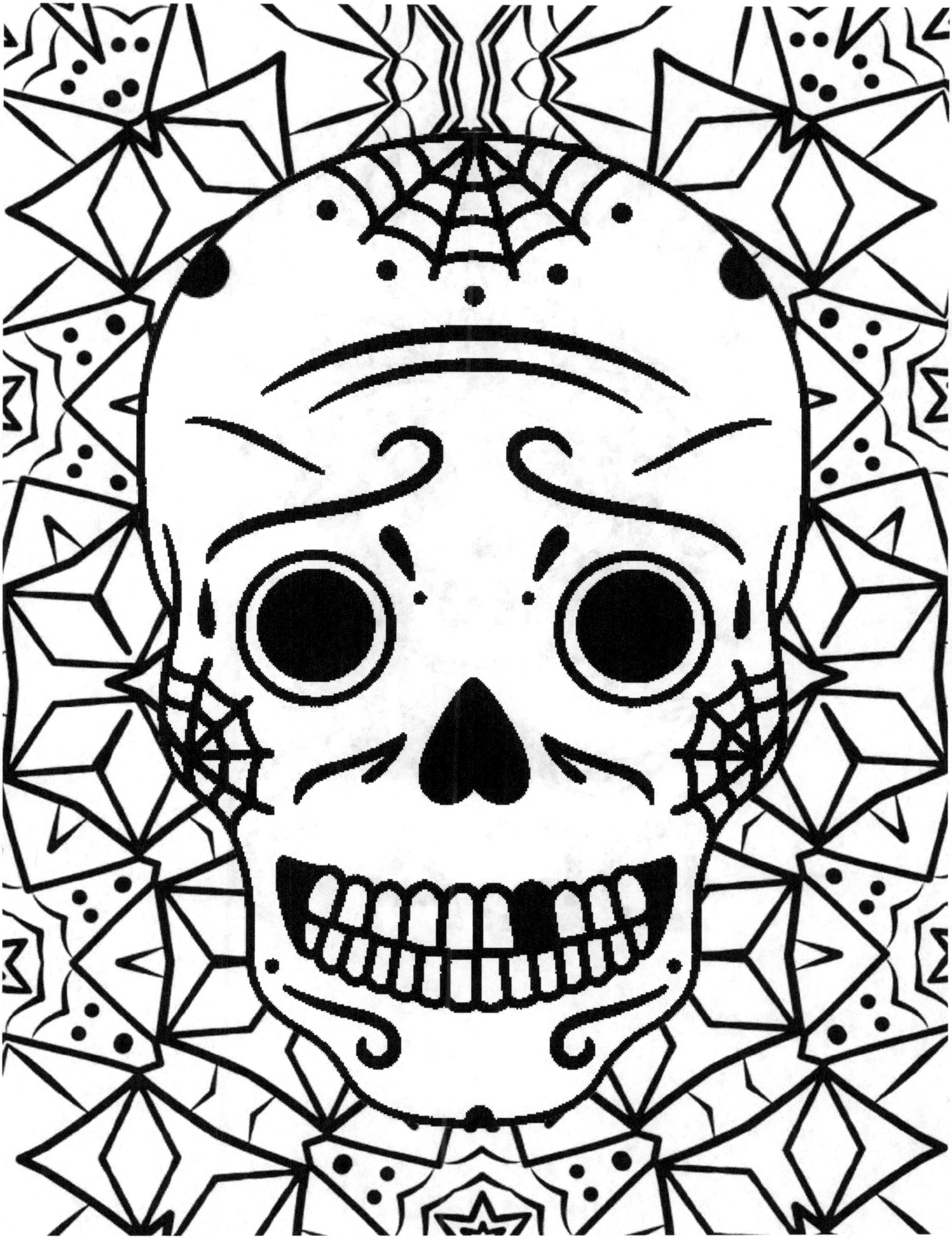

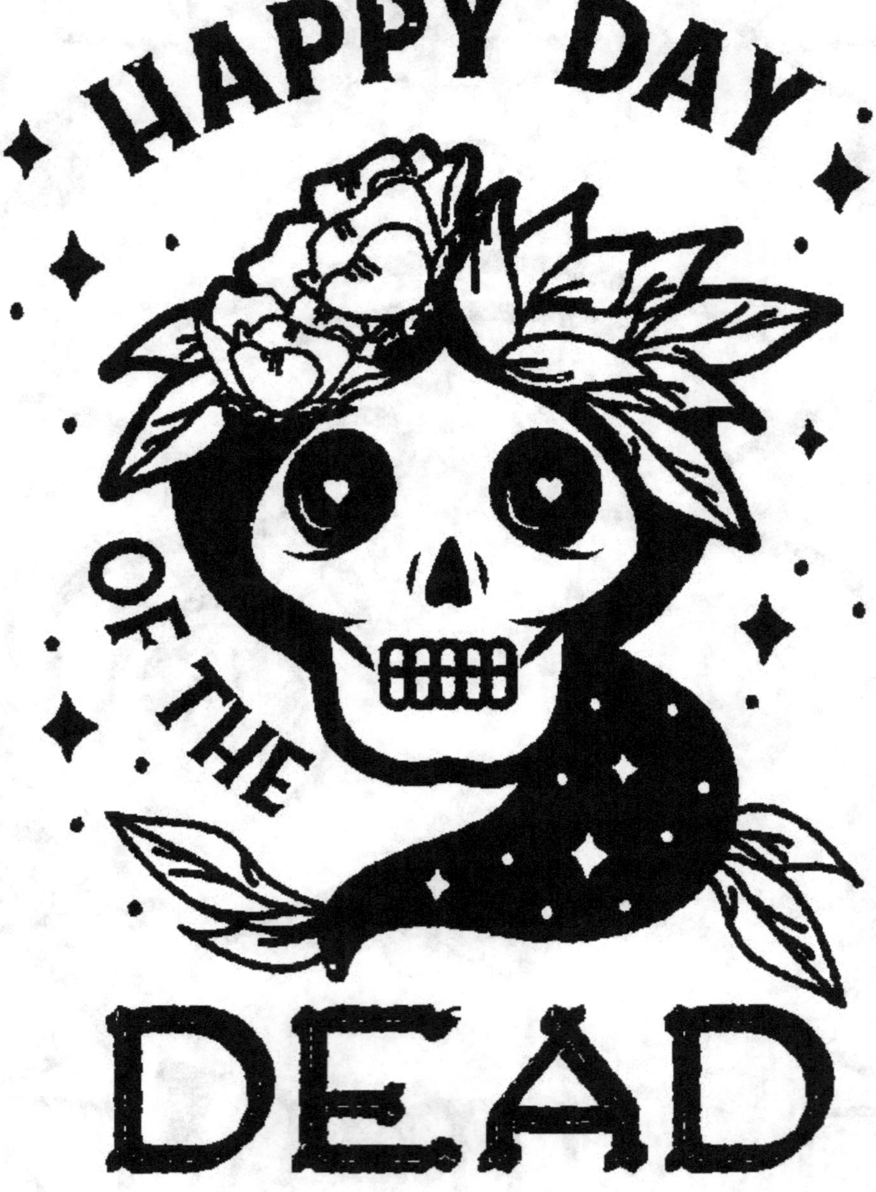
HAPPY DAY
OF THE
DEAD

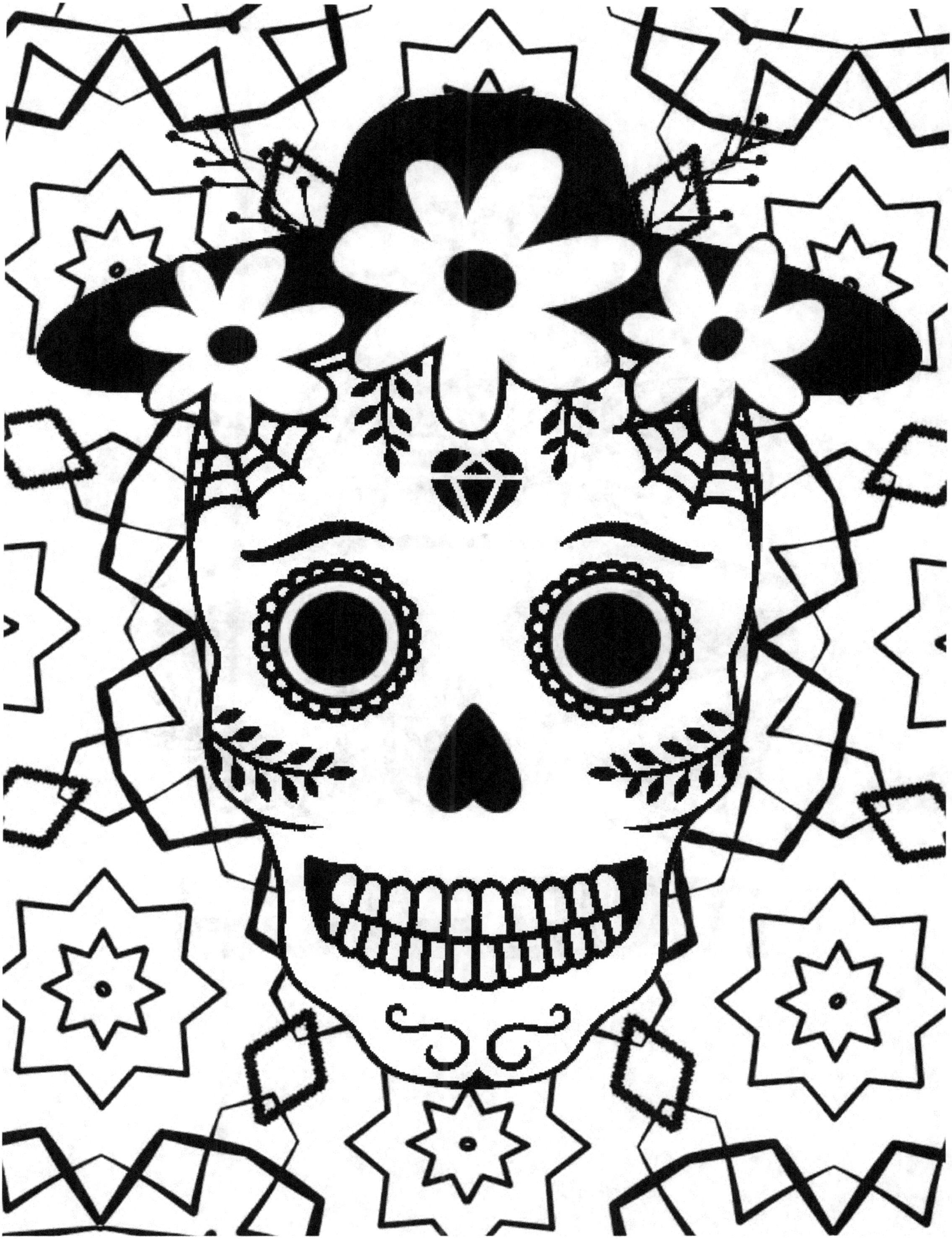

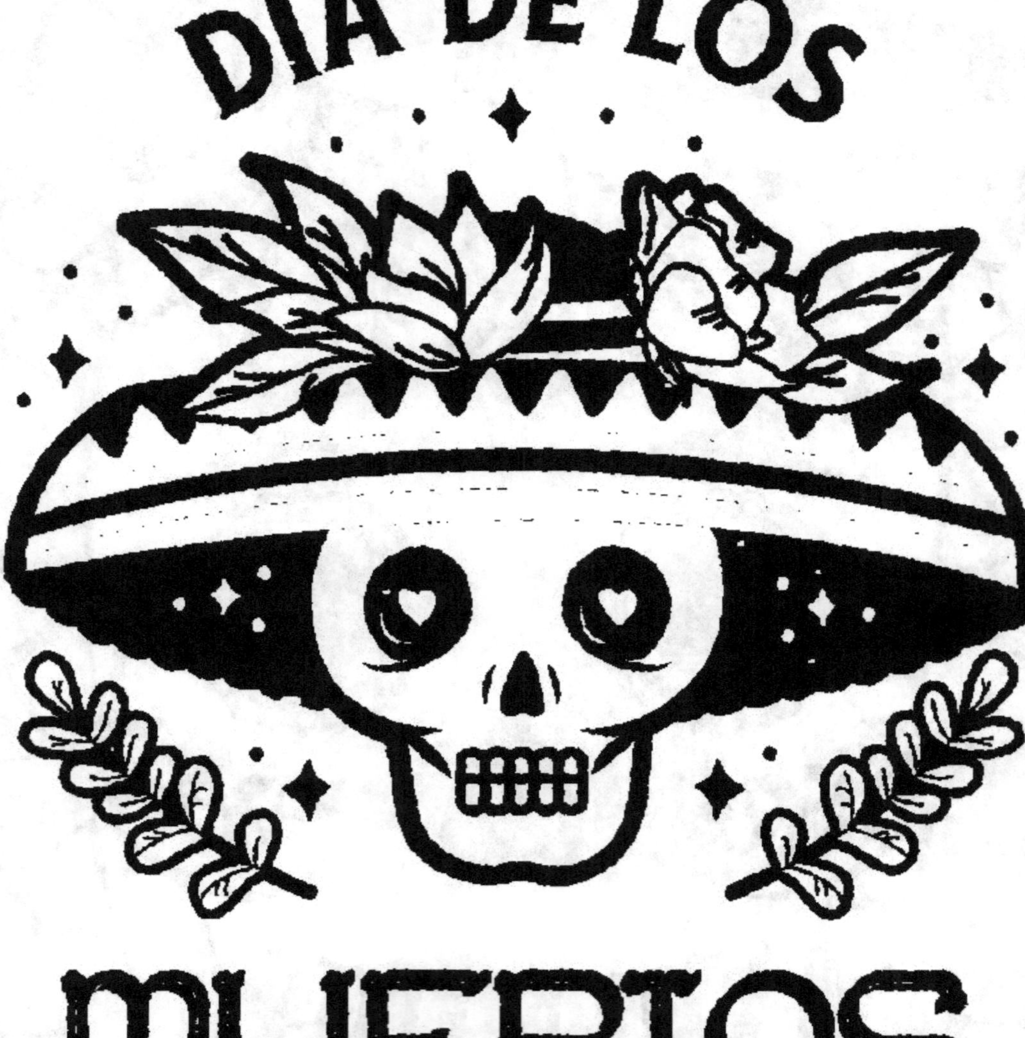
DIA DE LOS
MUERTOS

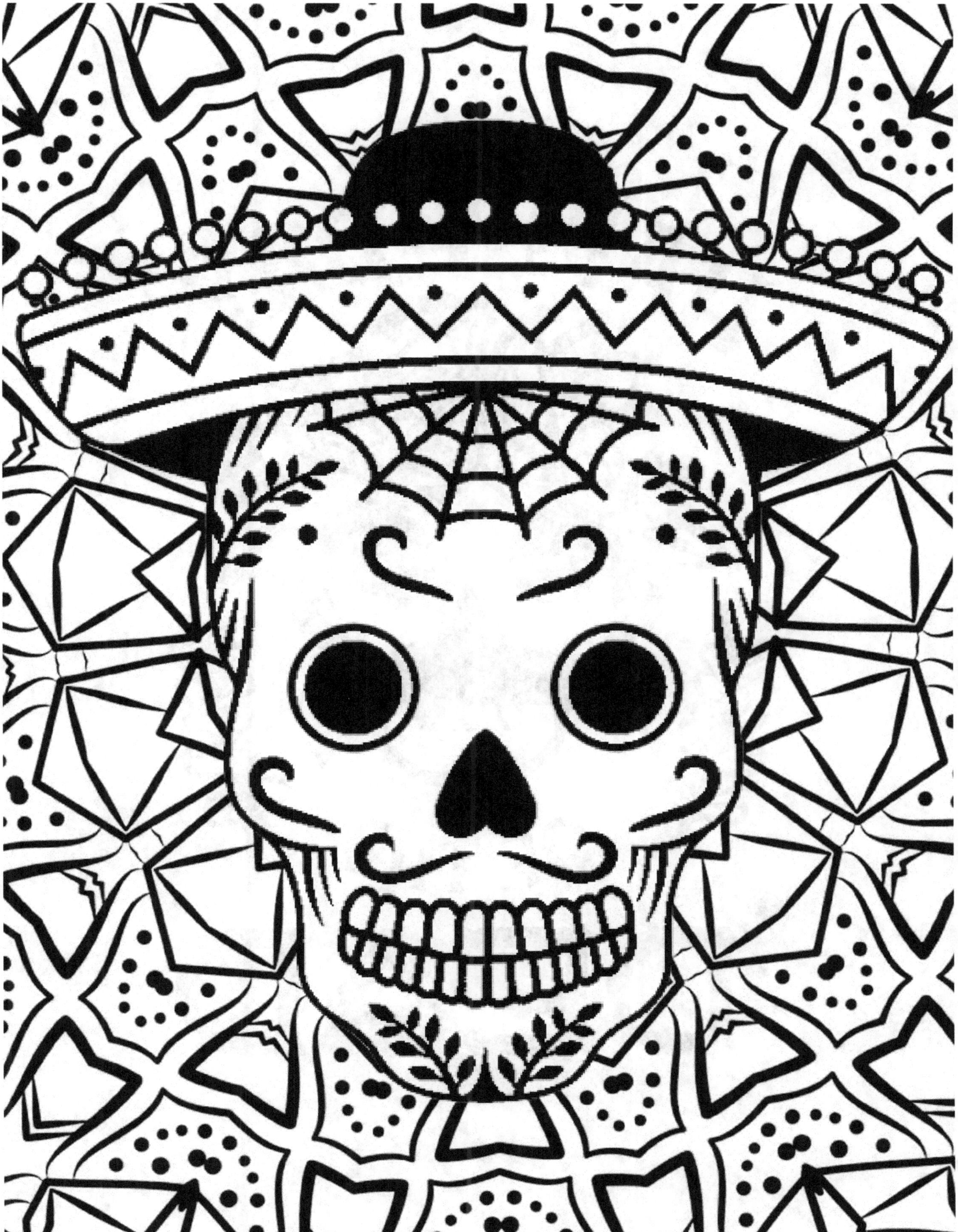

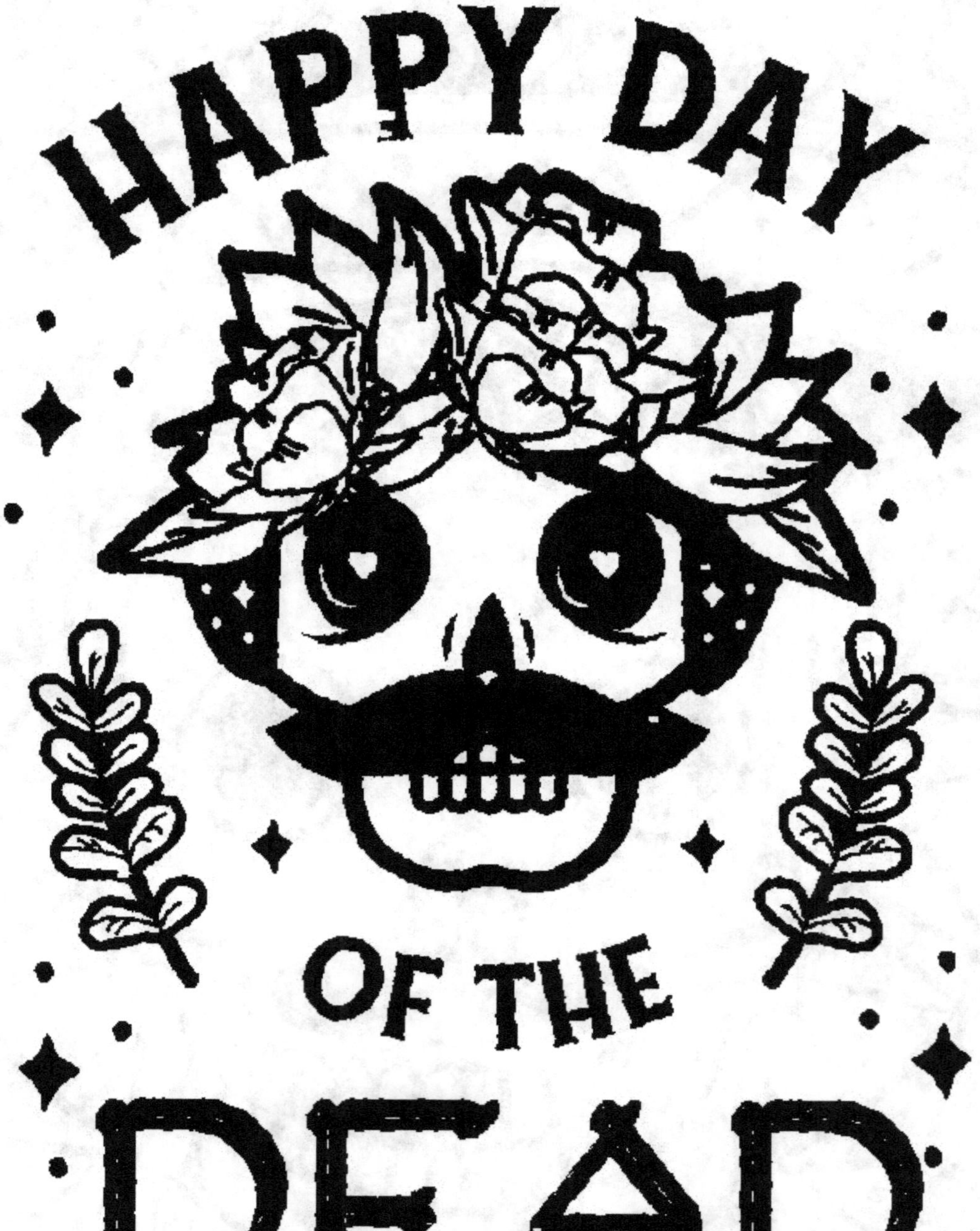
HAPPY DAY
OF THE
DEAD

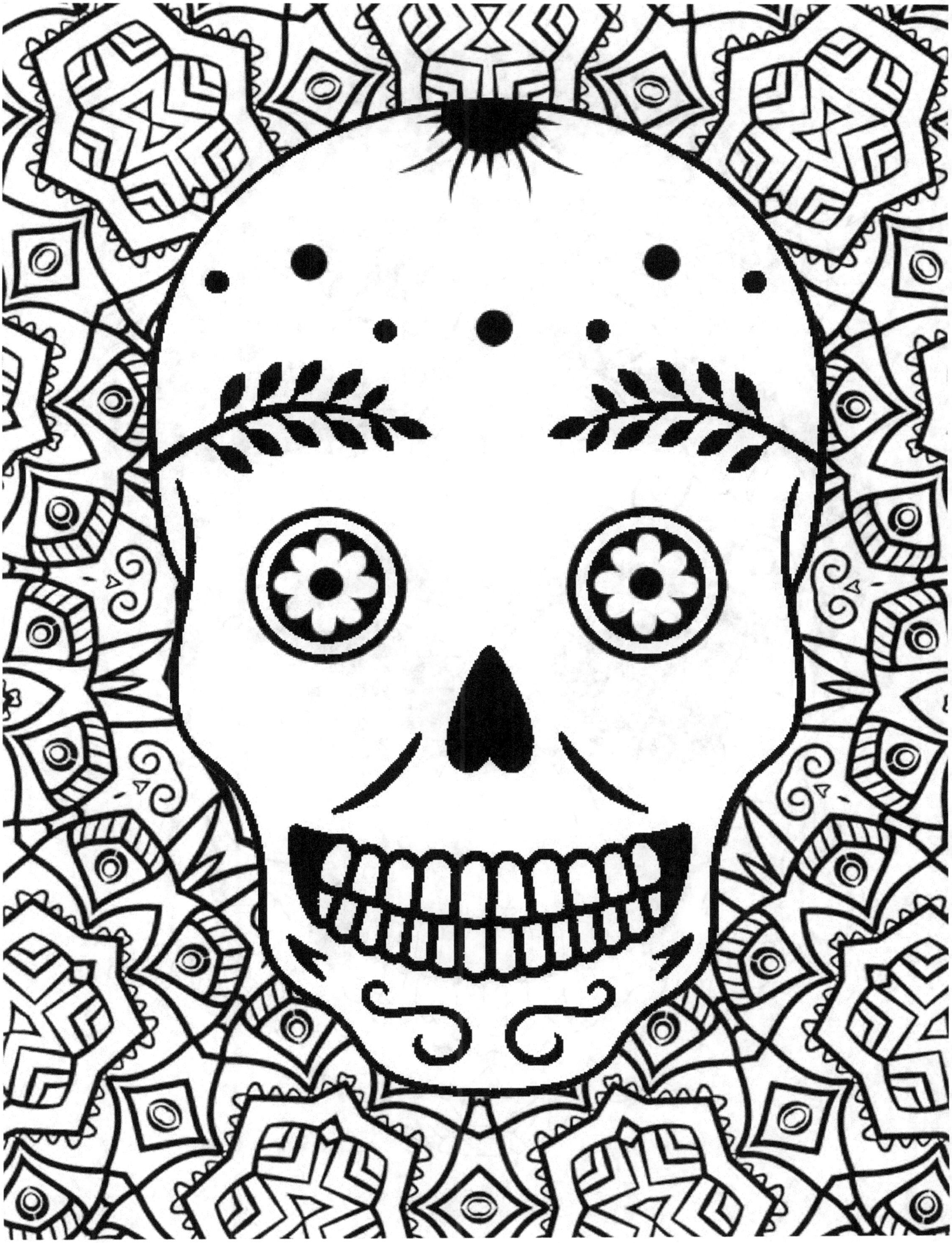

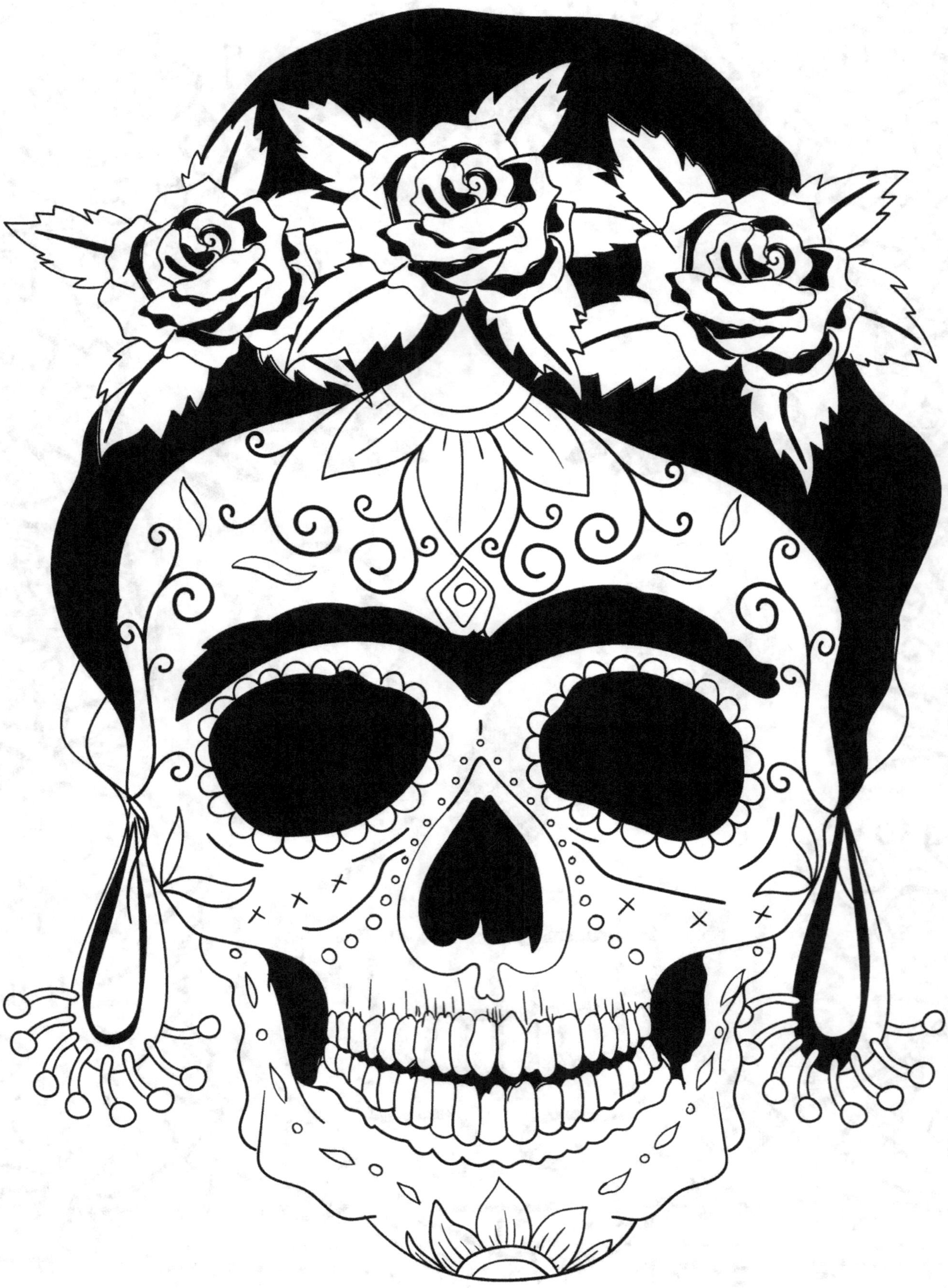

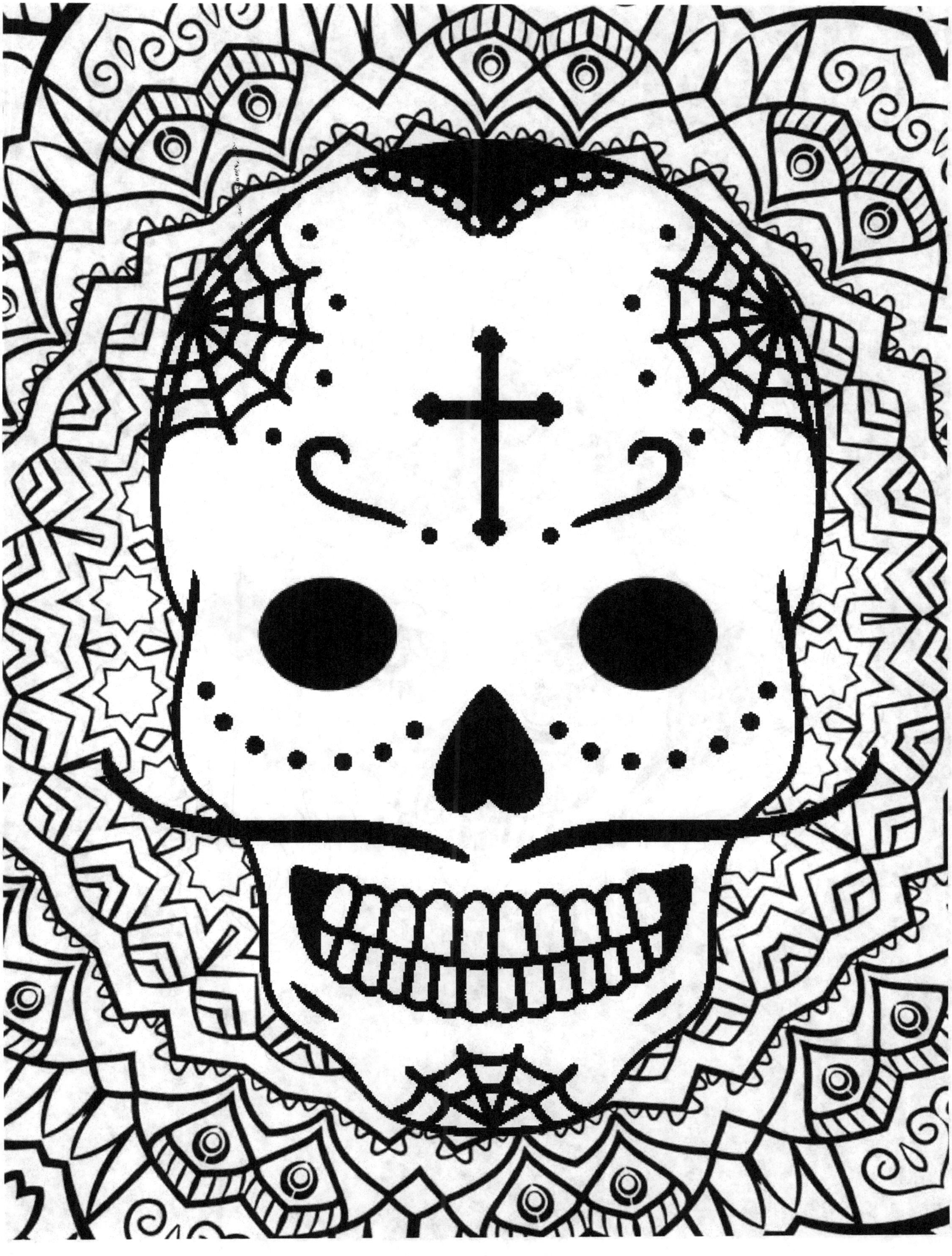

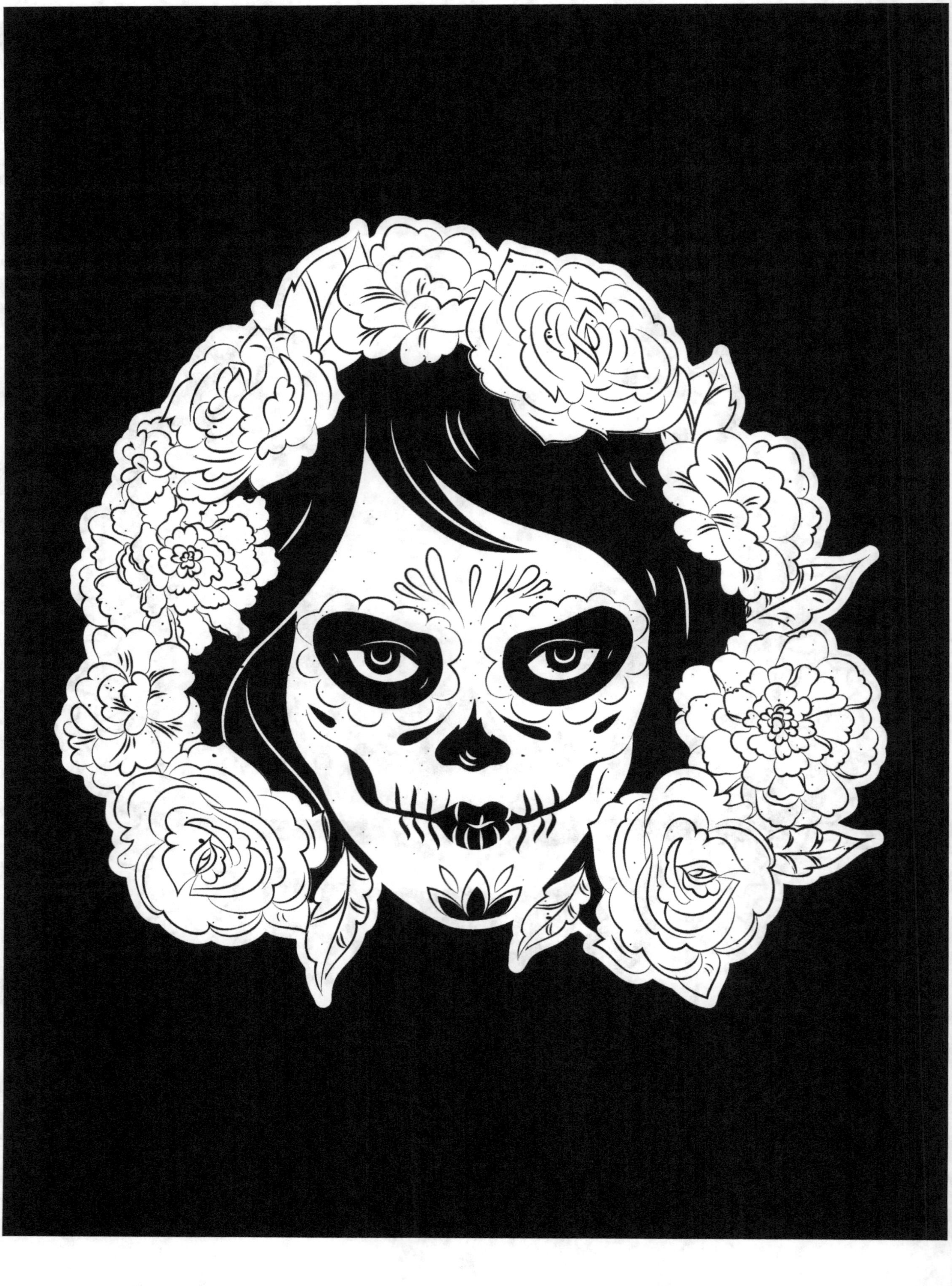

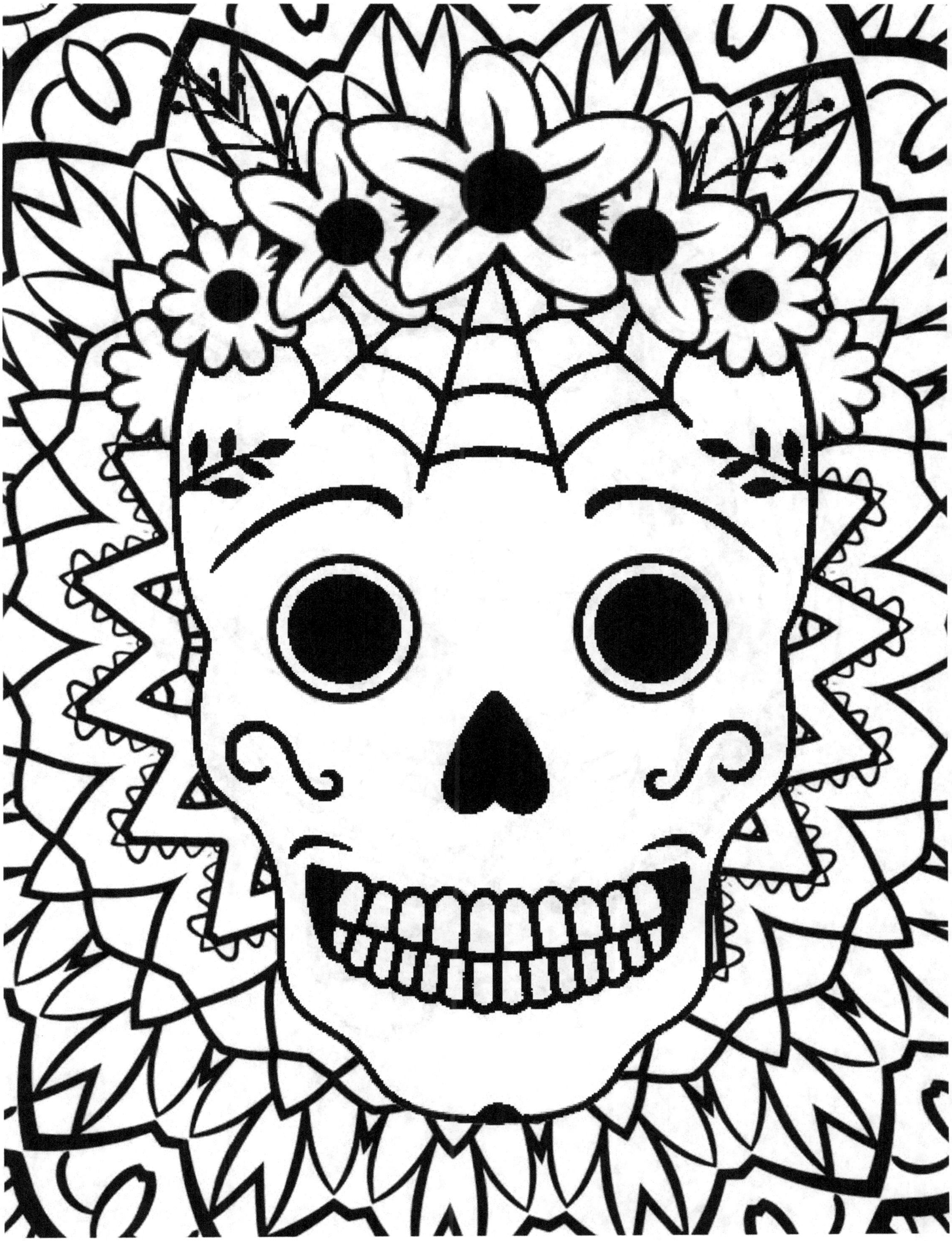

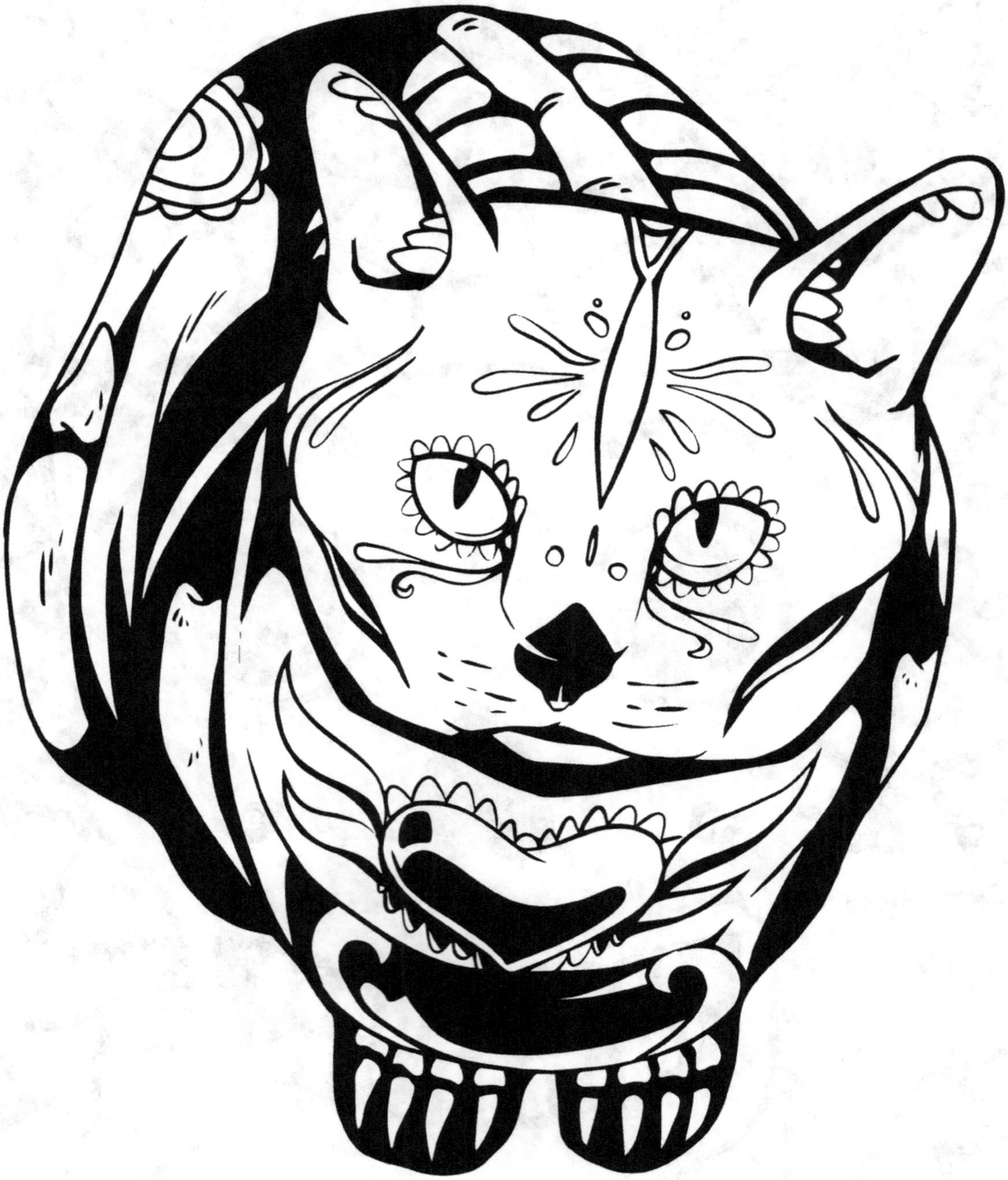

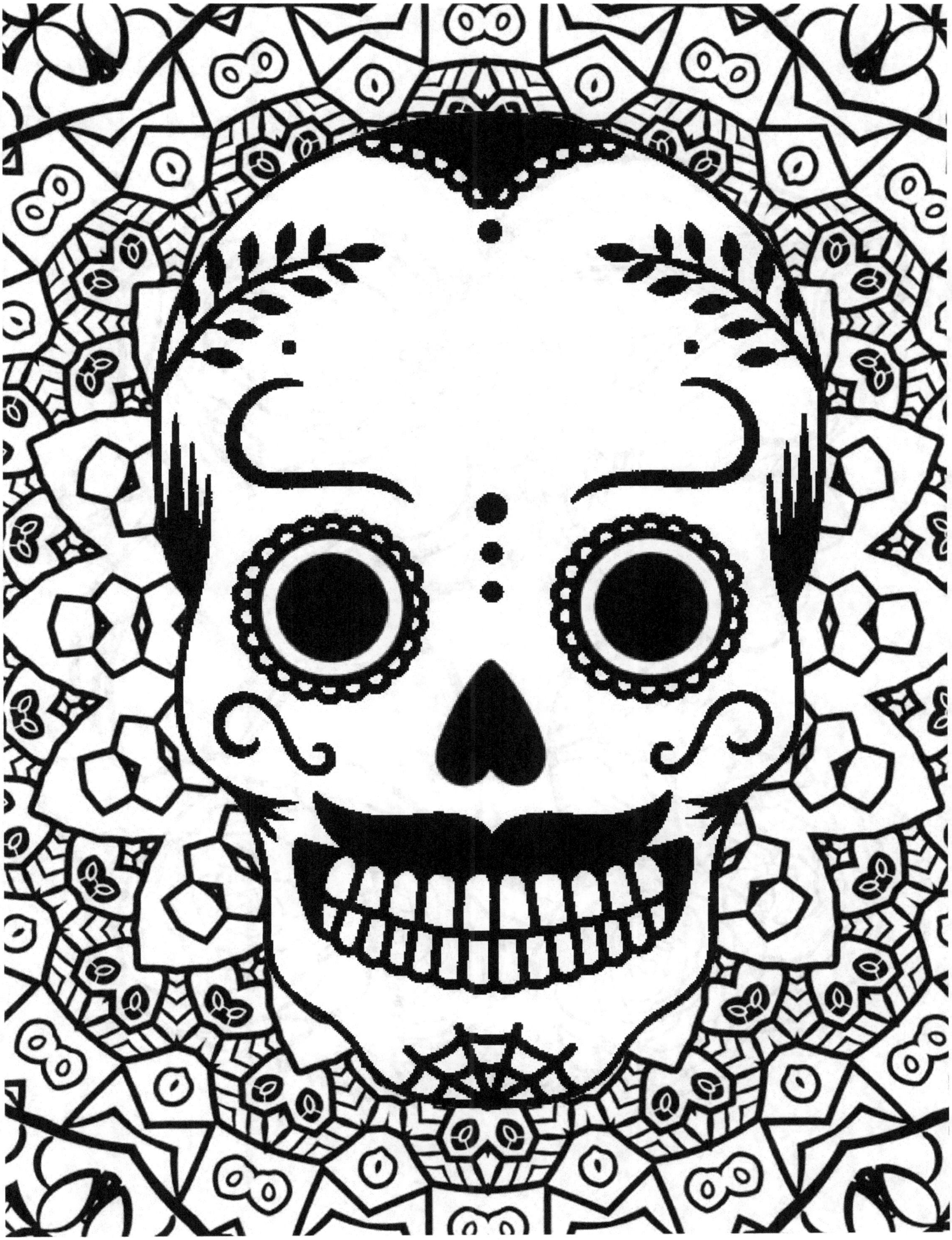

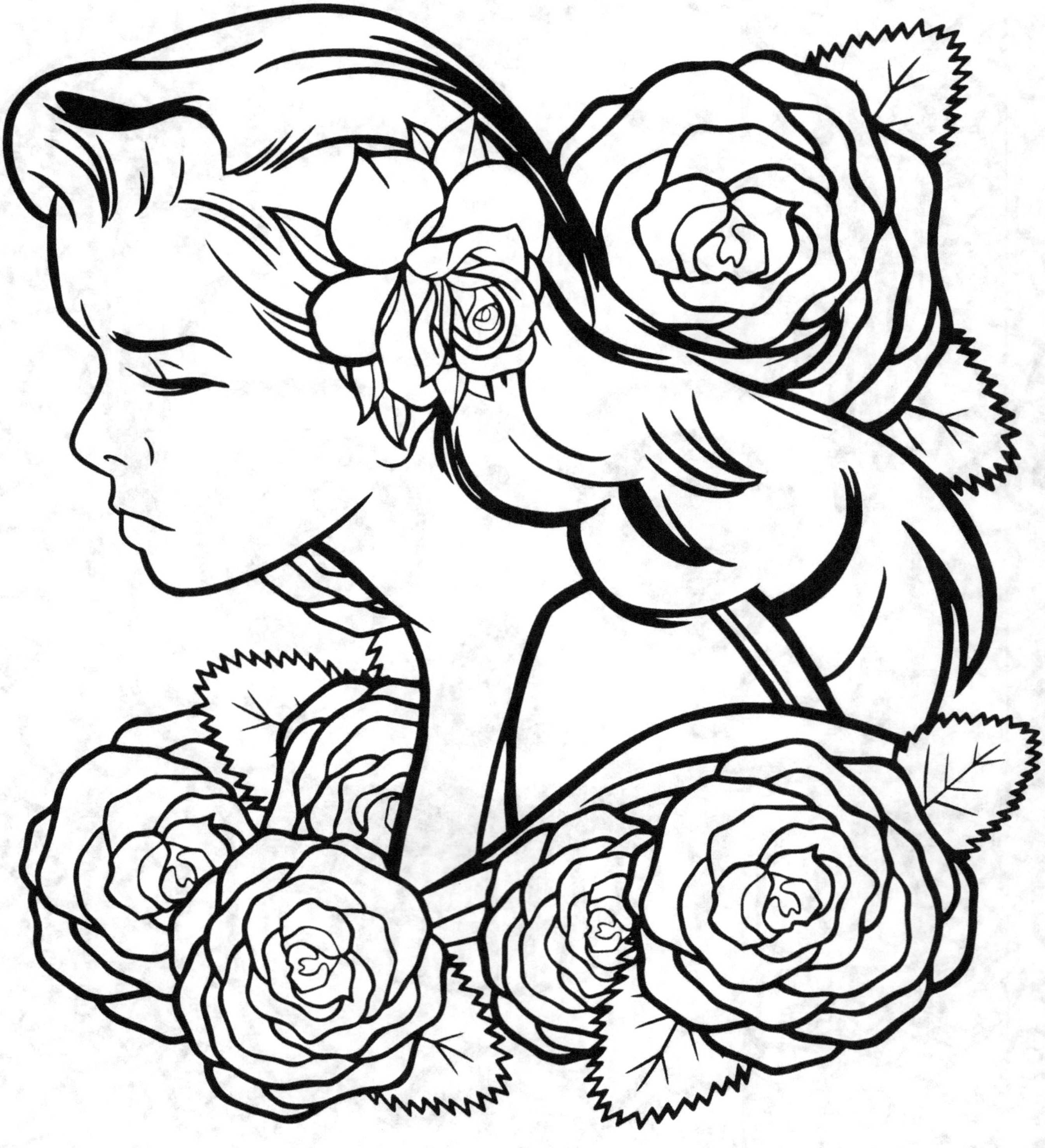

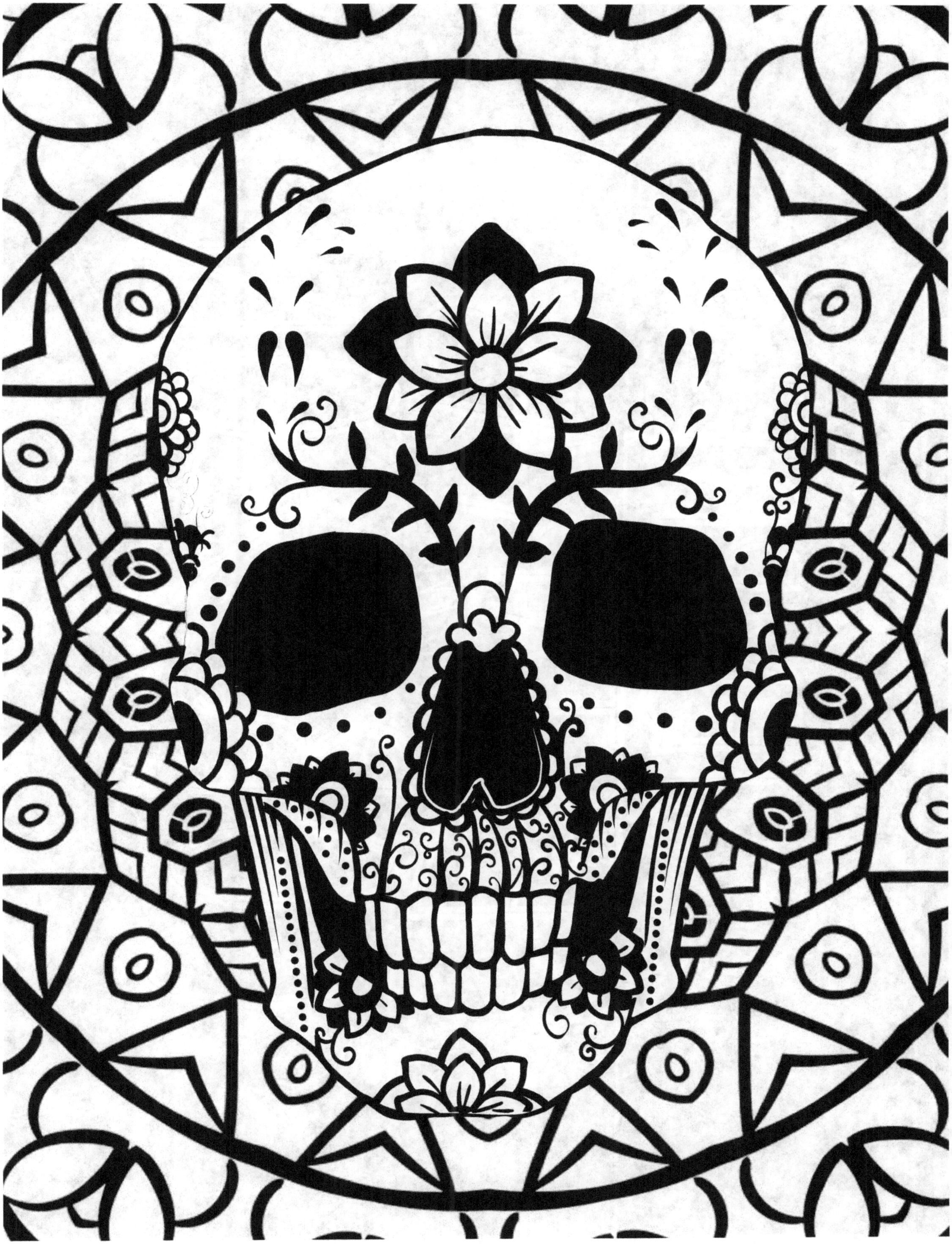

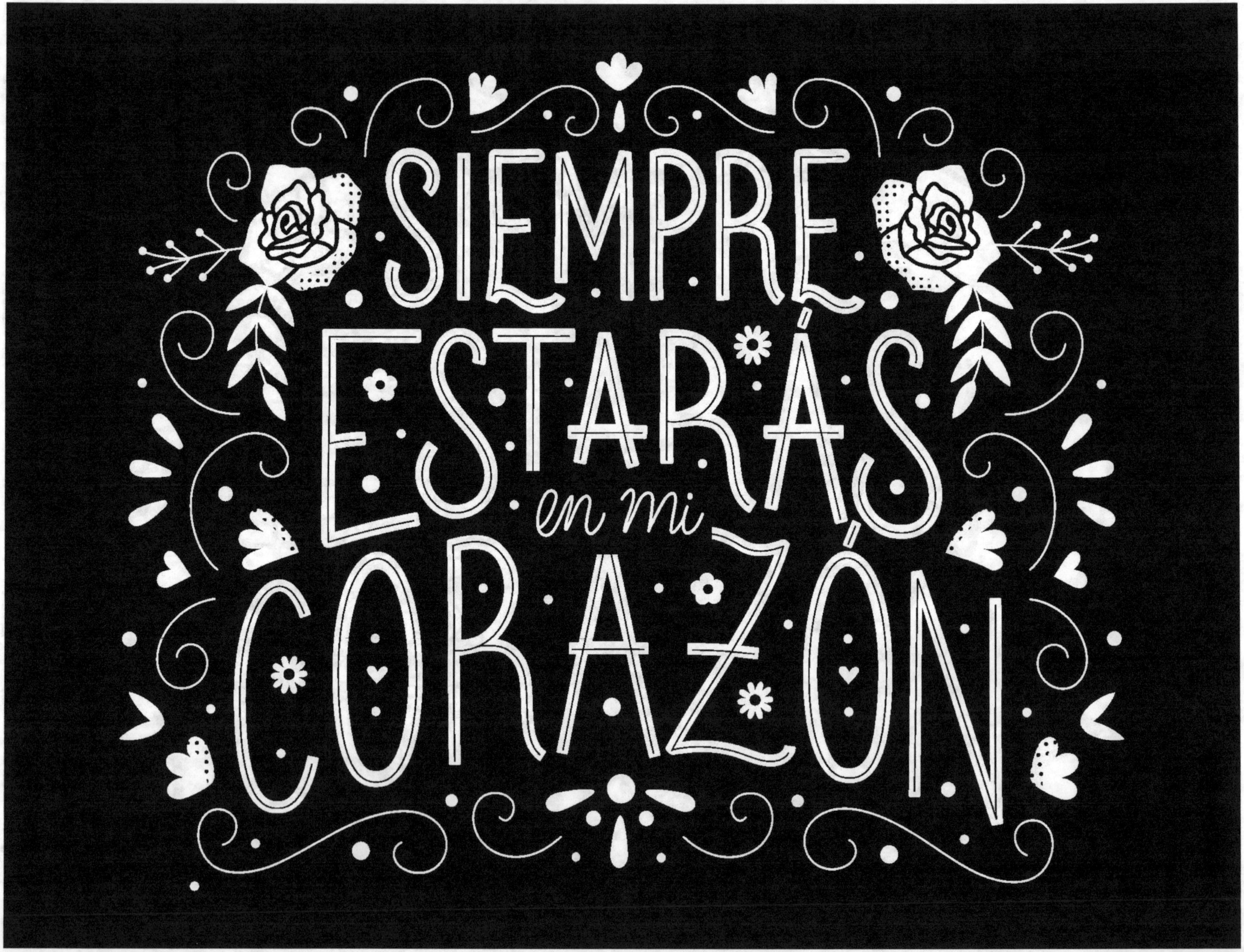
SIEMPRE
ESTARÁS
en mi
CORAZÓN

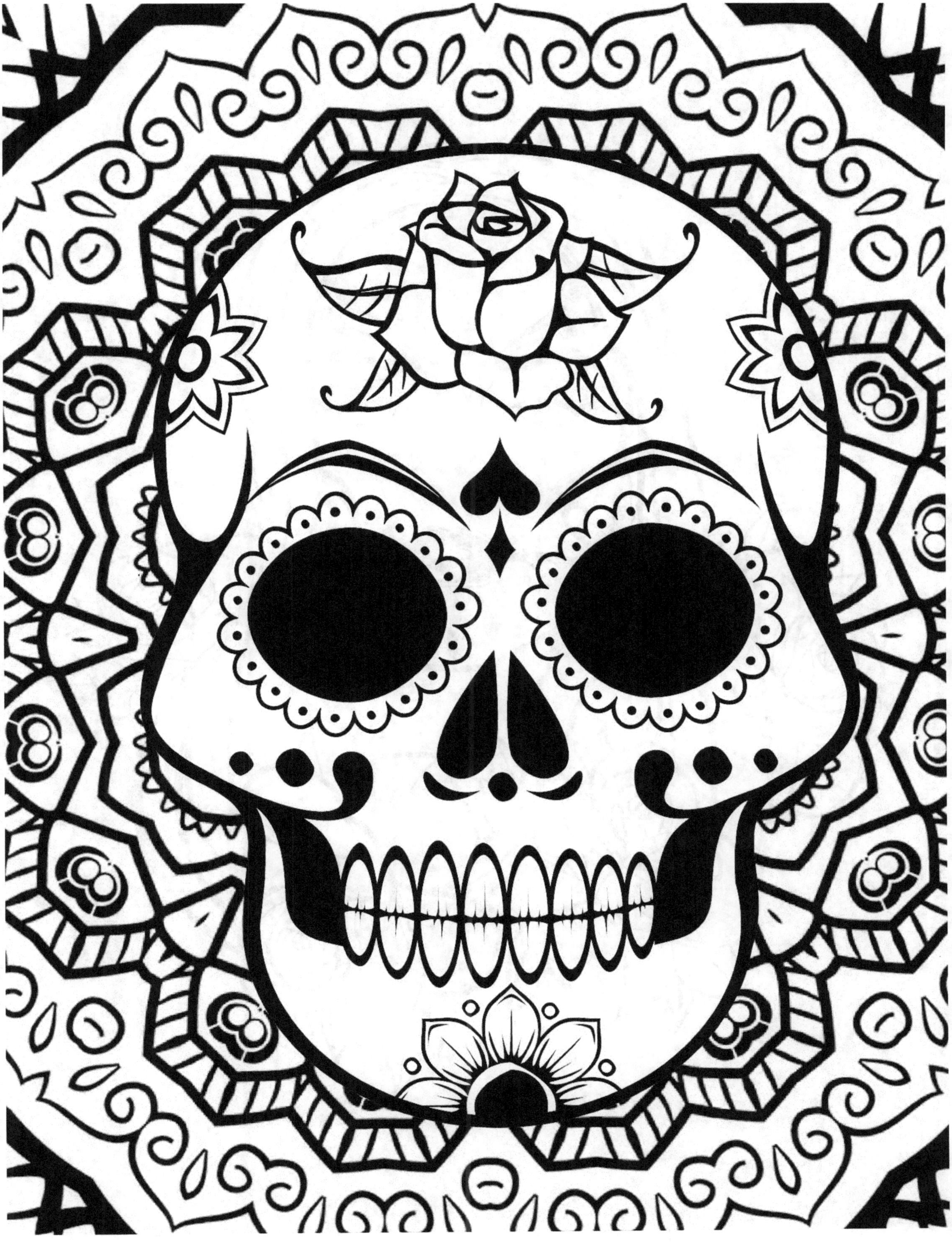

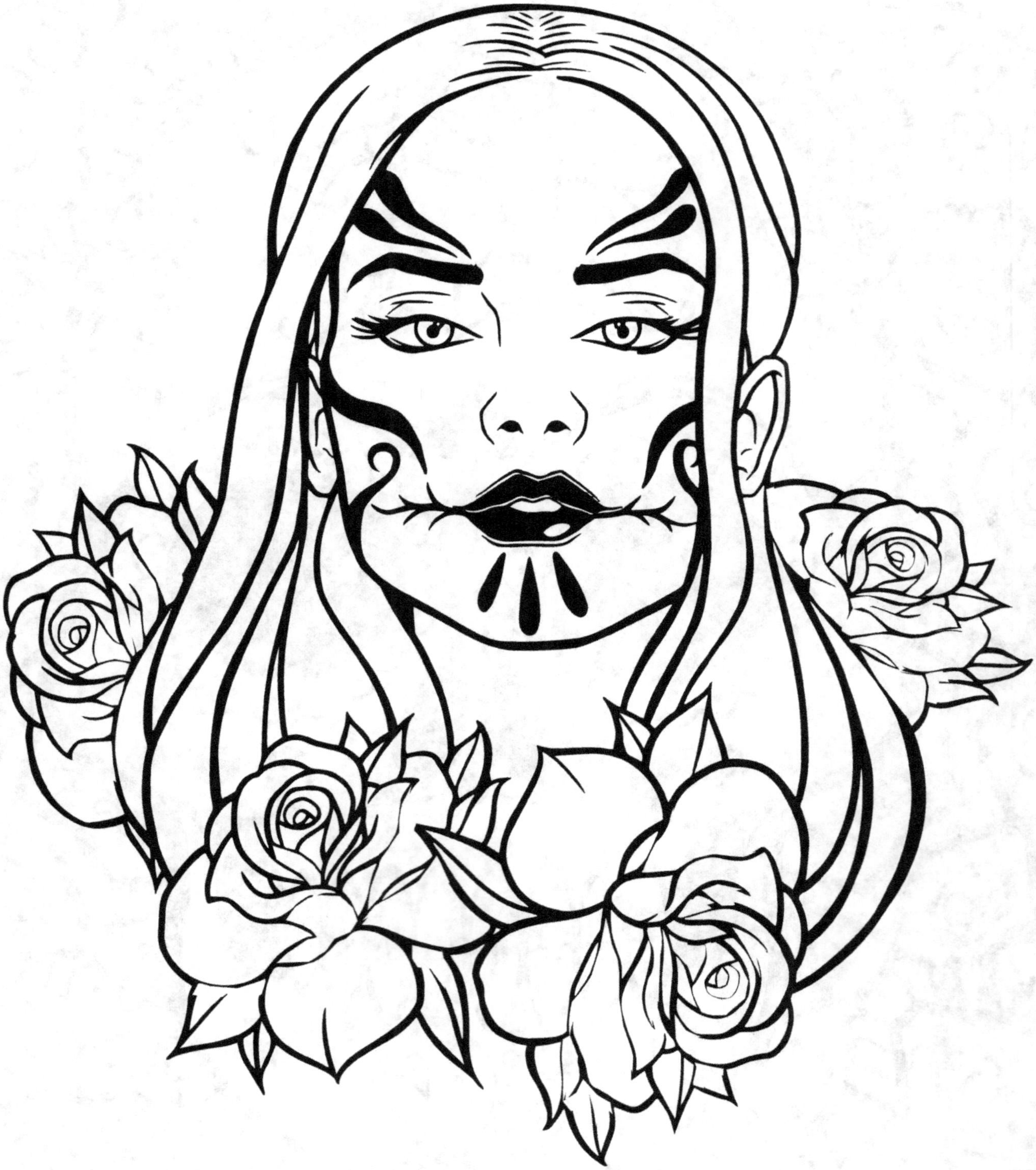

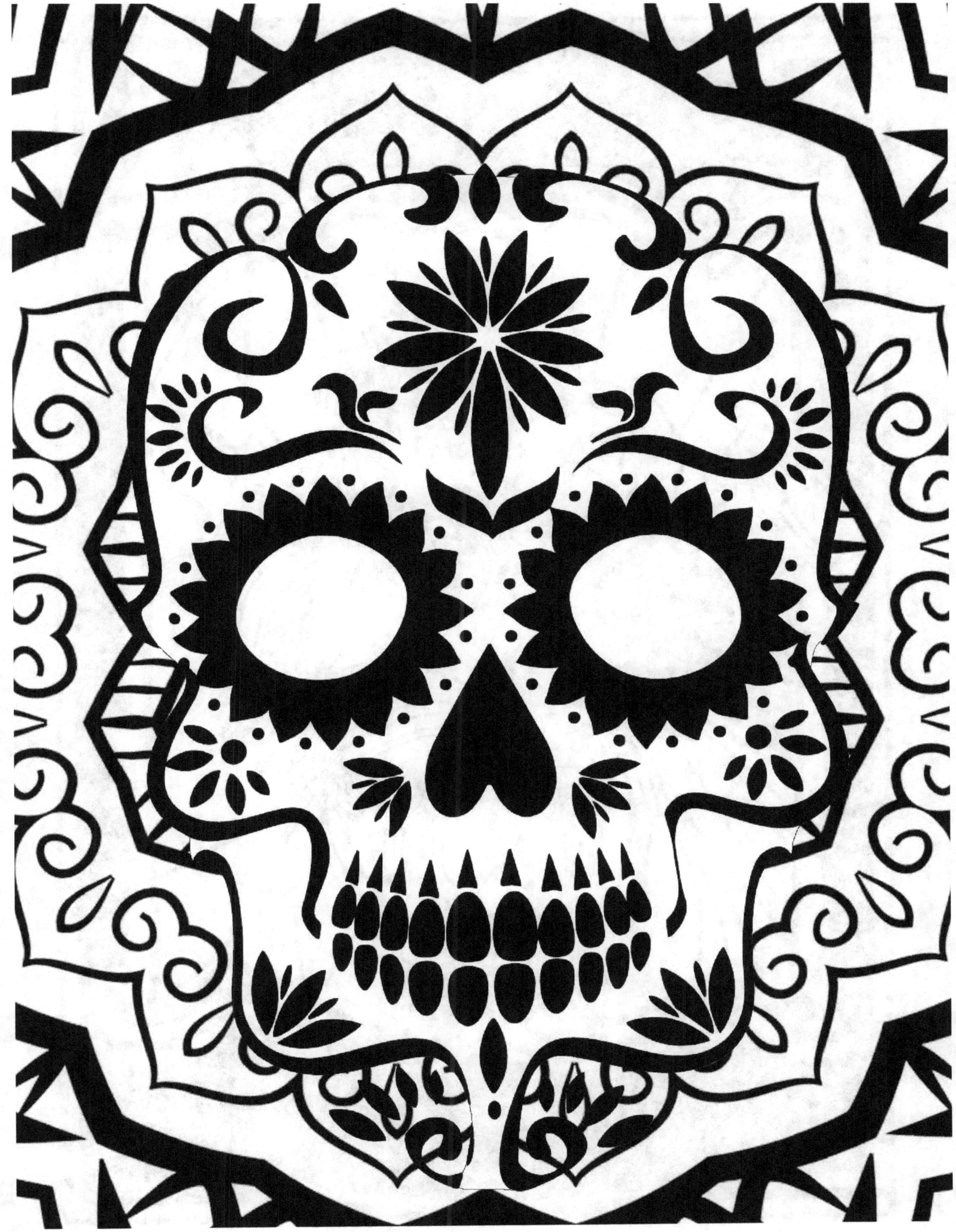

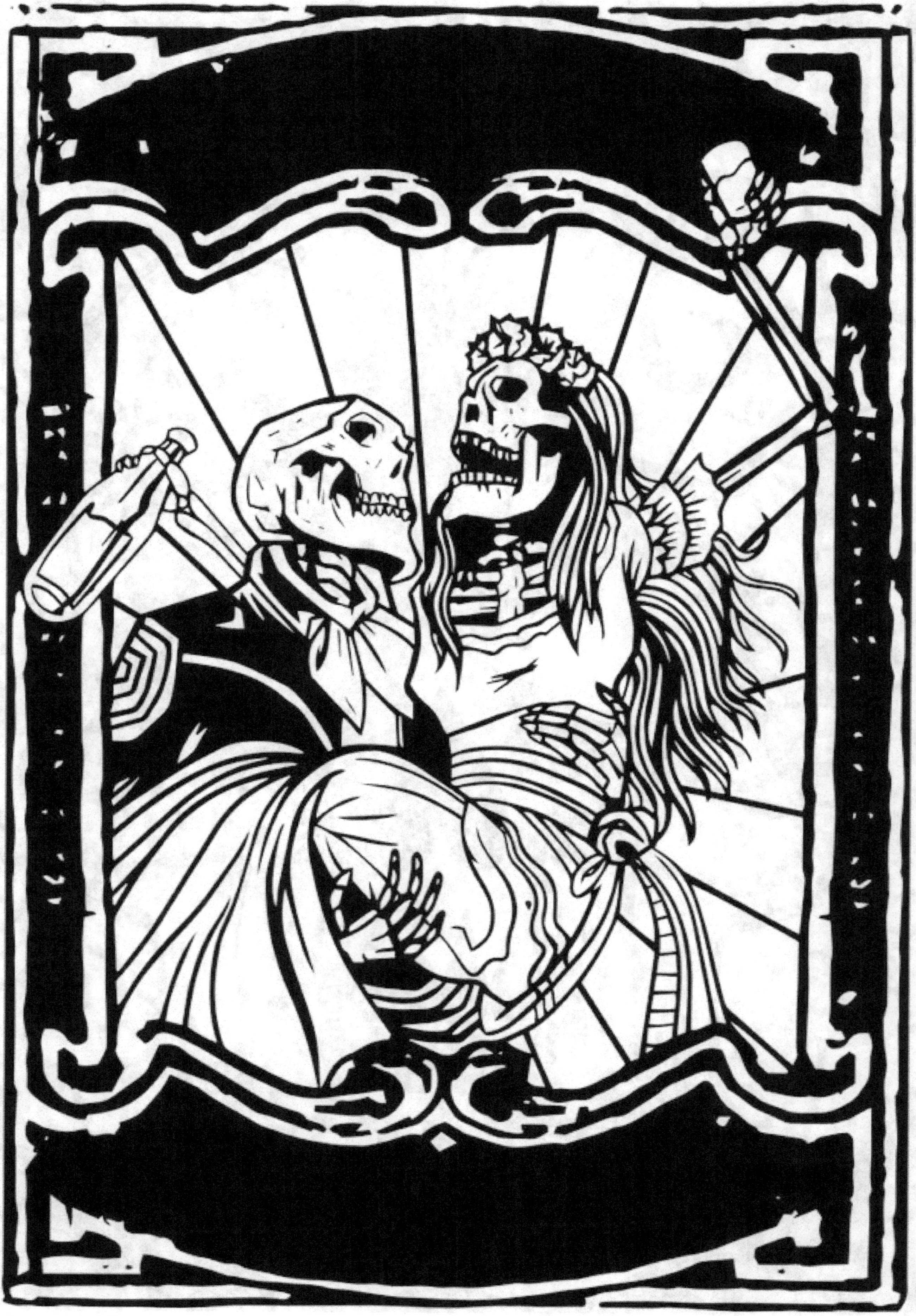

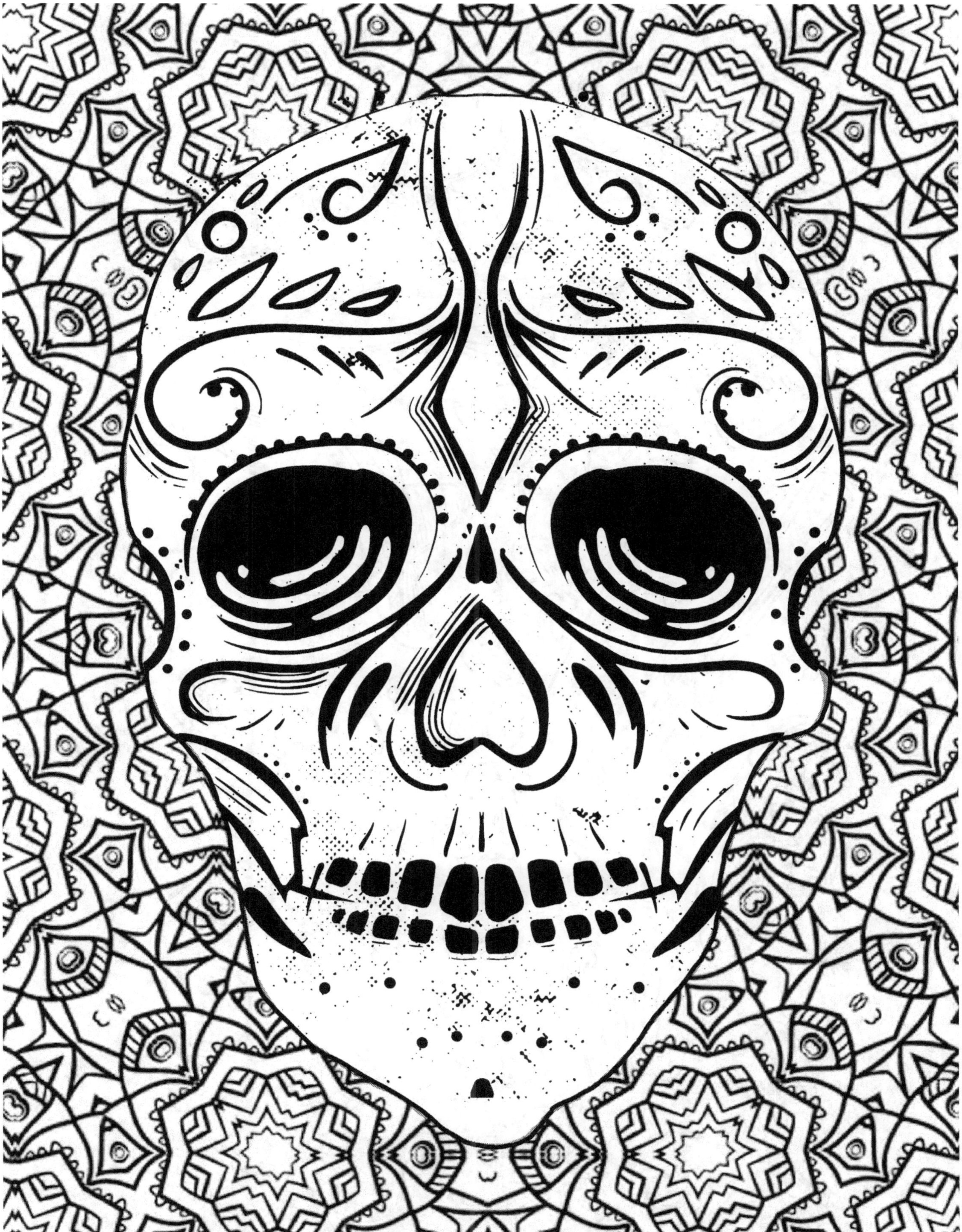

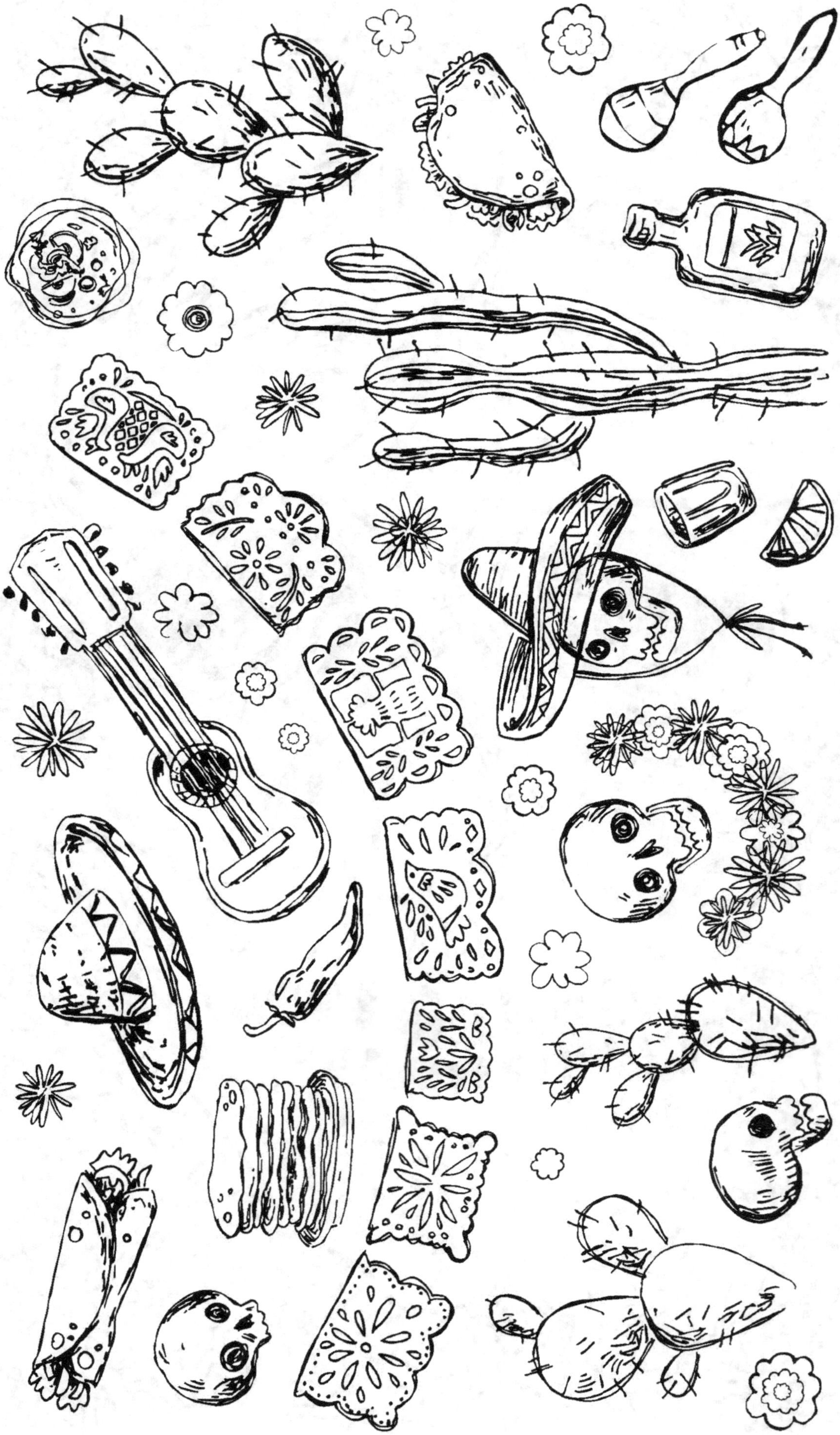

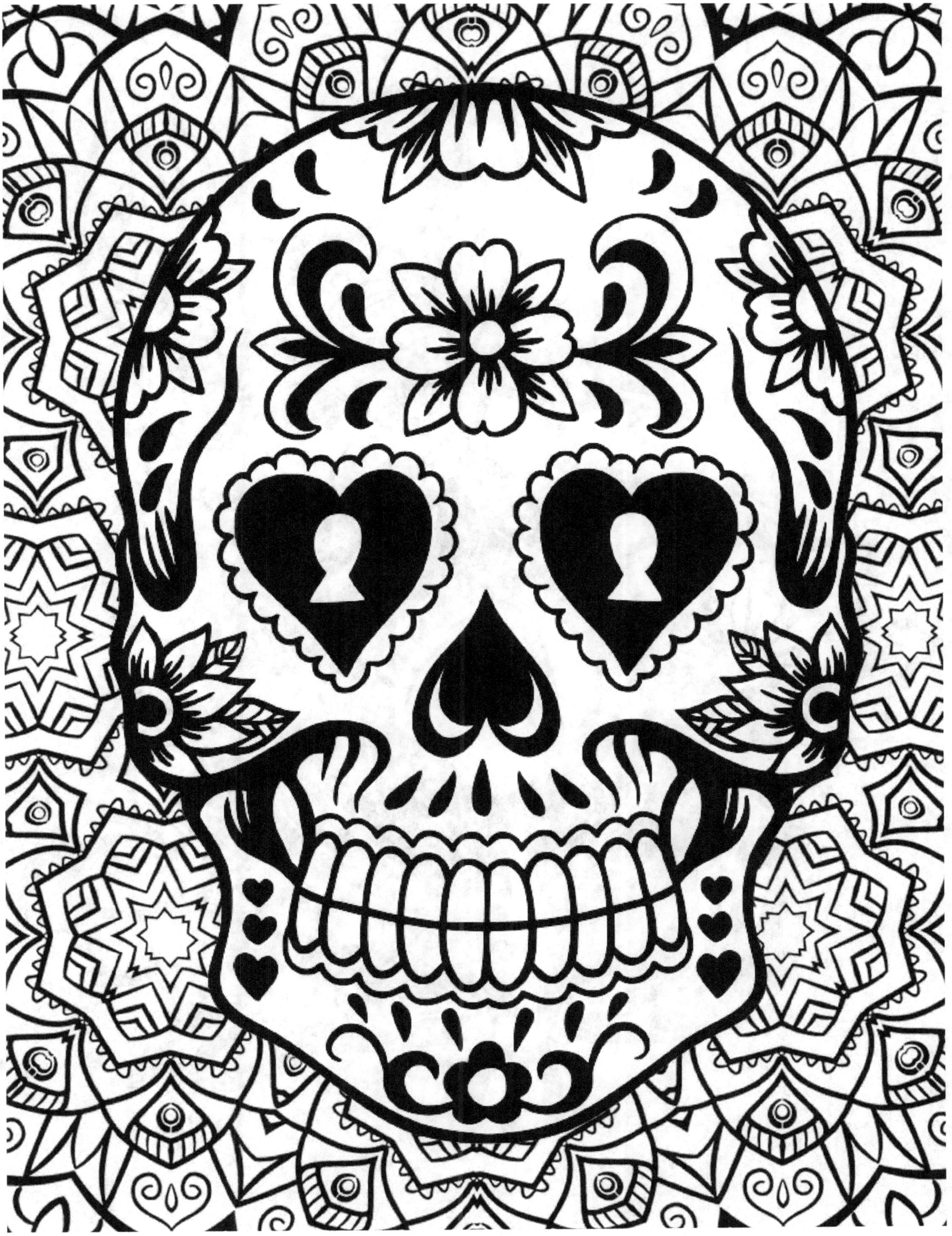

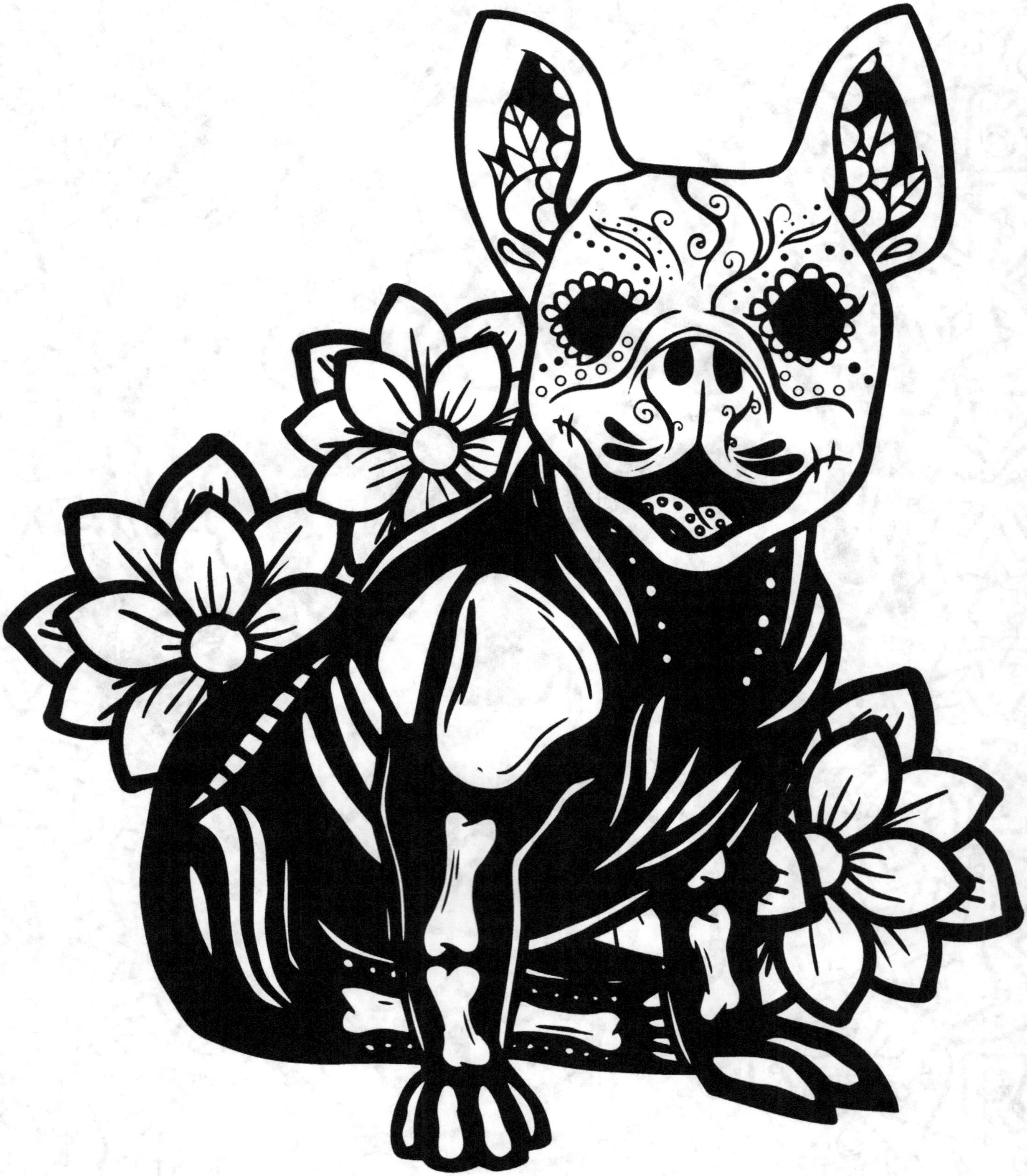

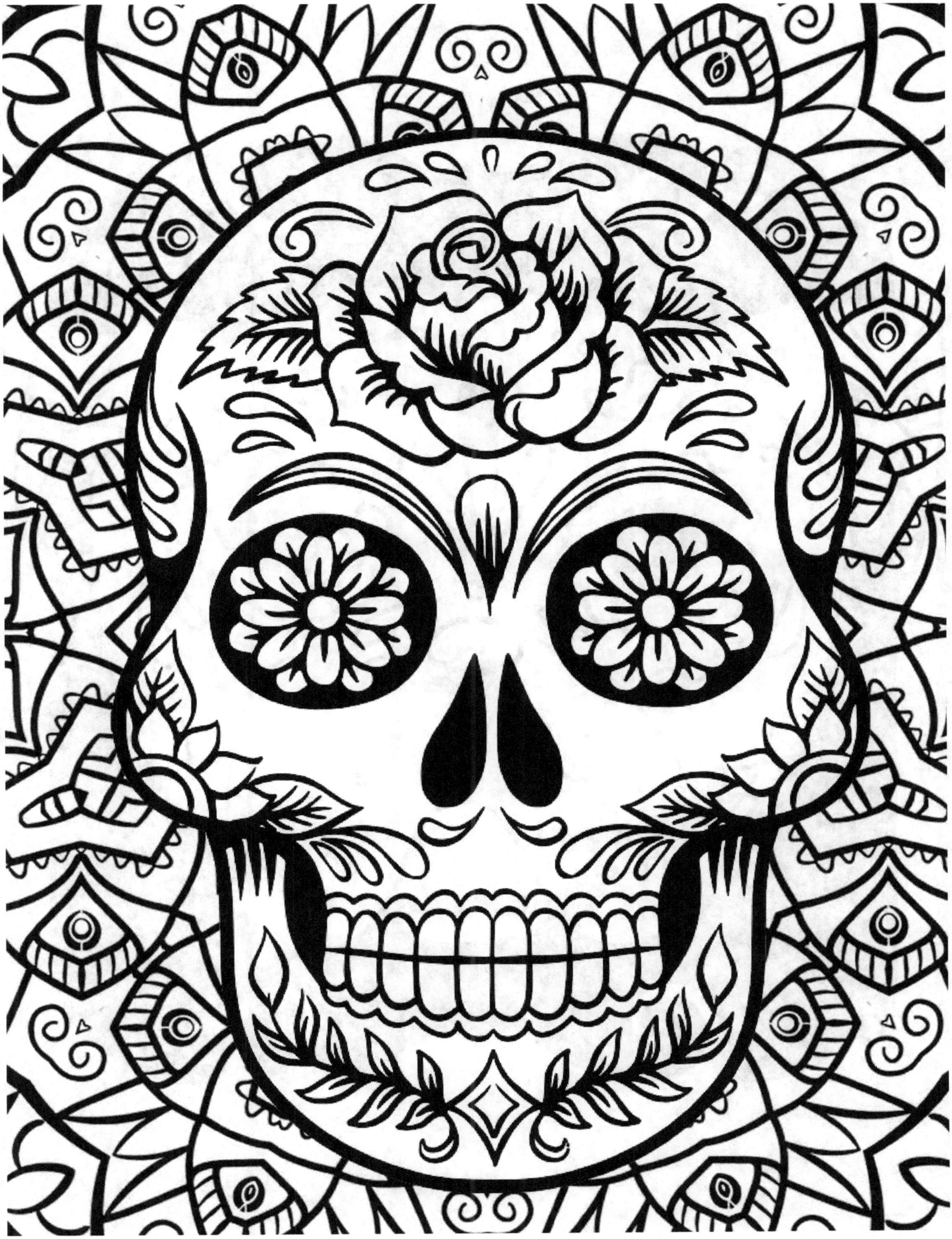

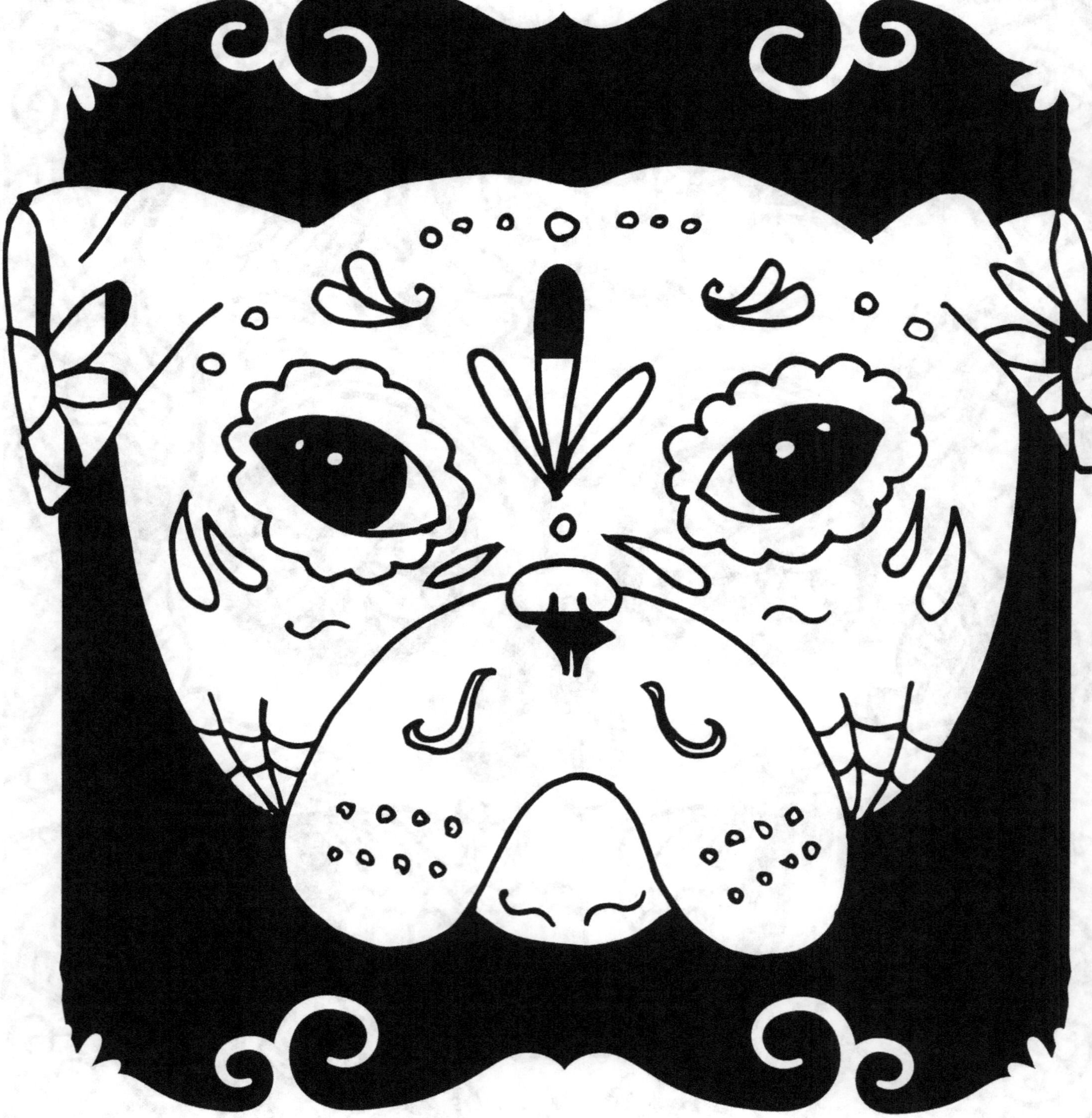

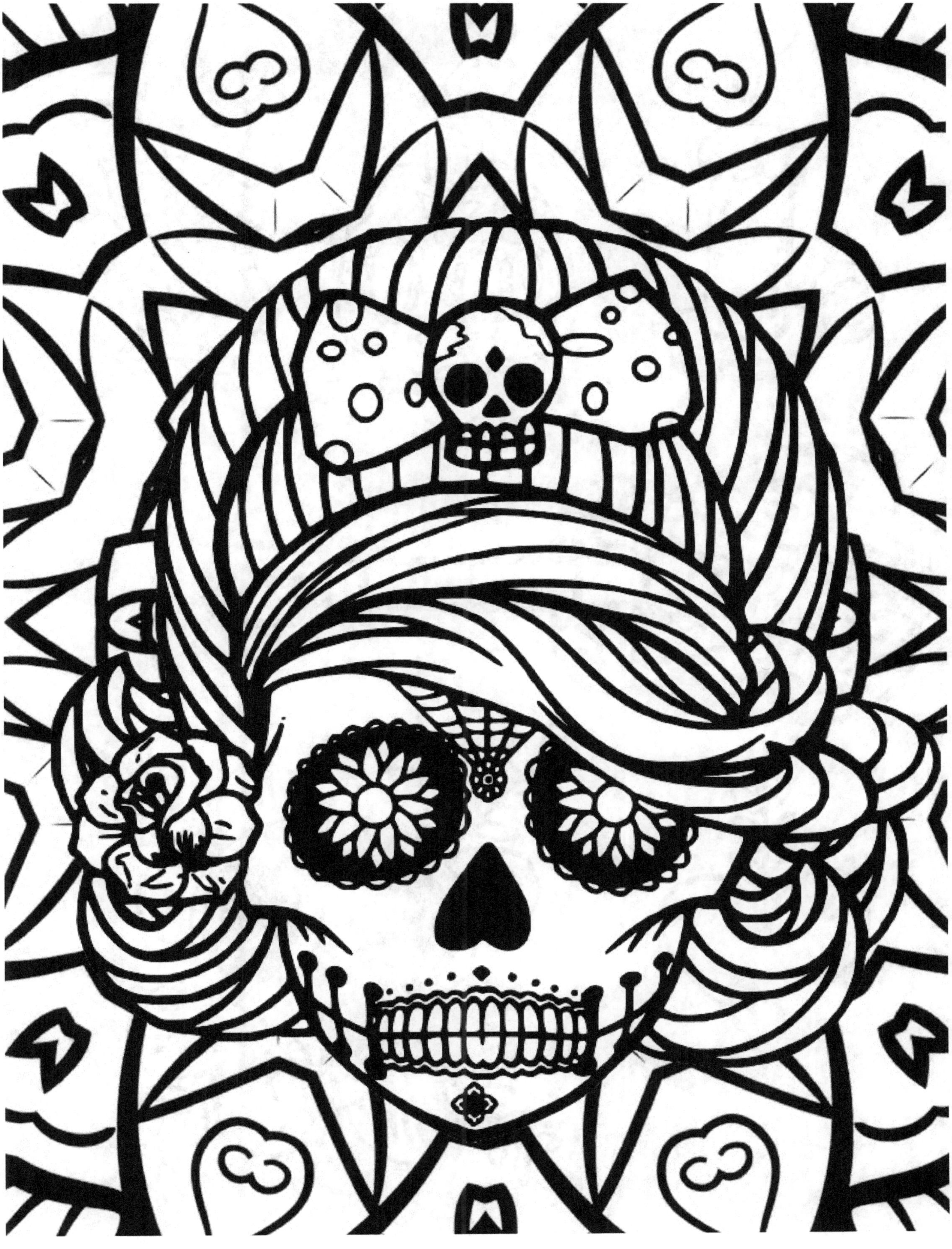

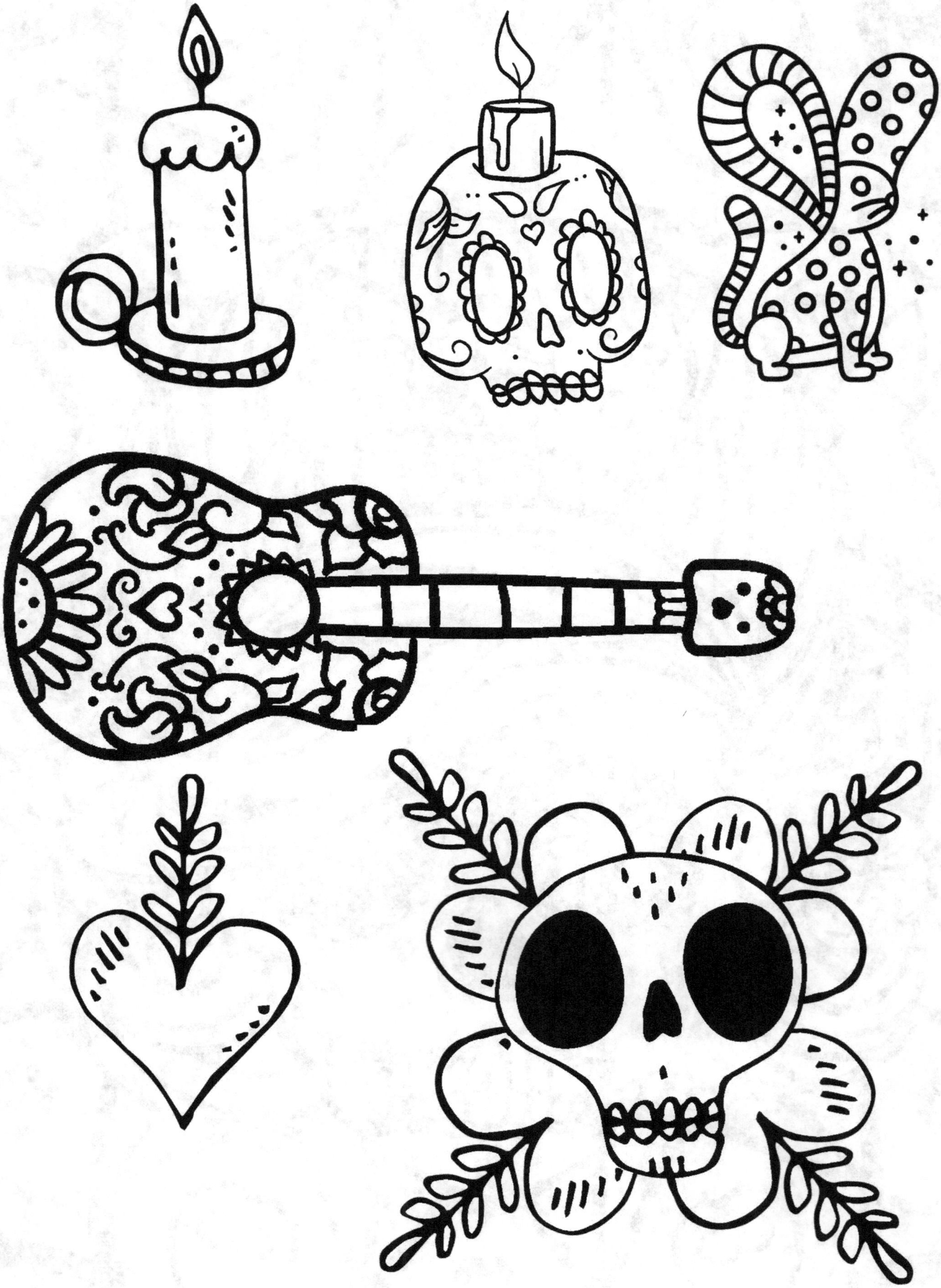

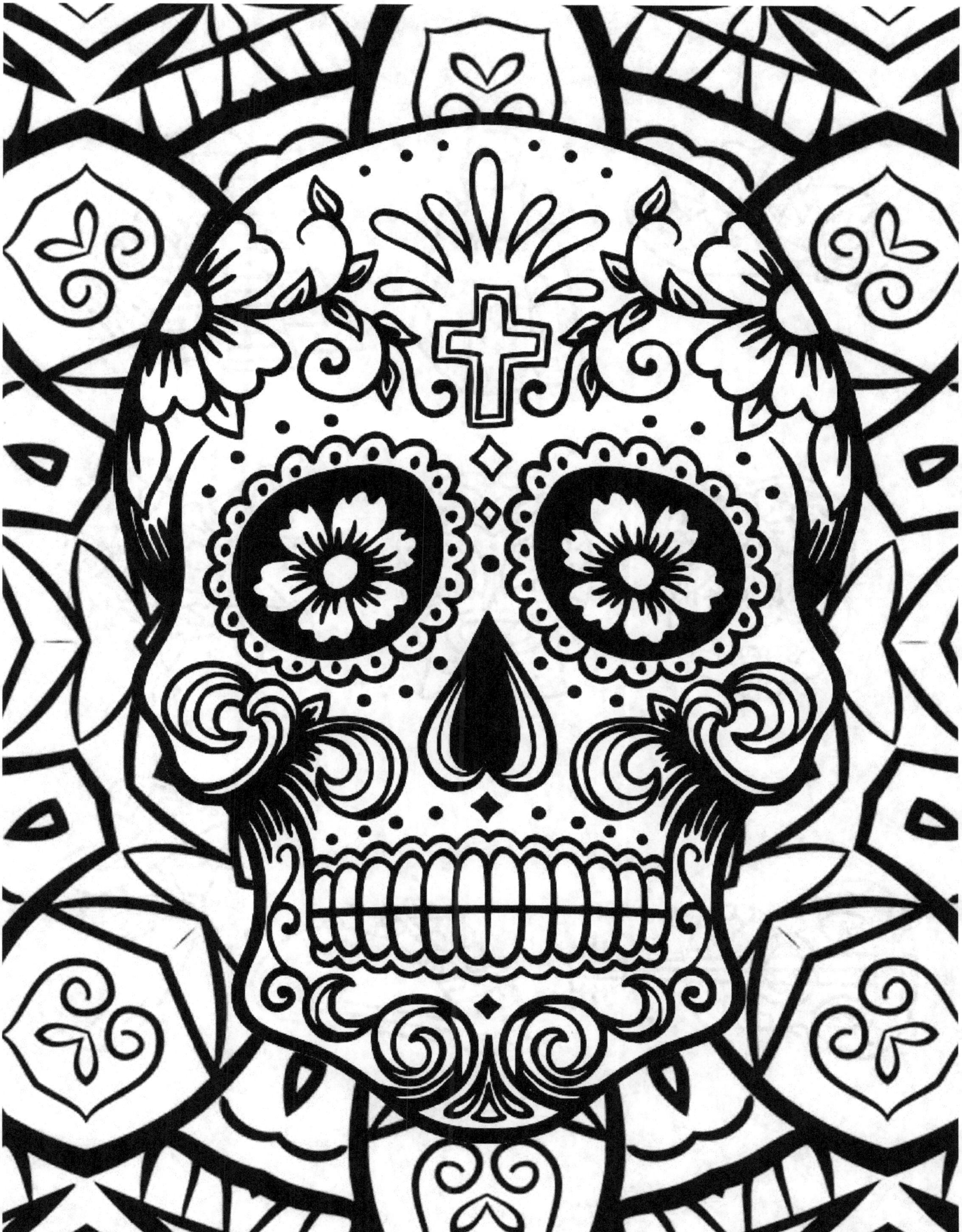

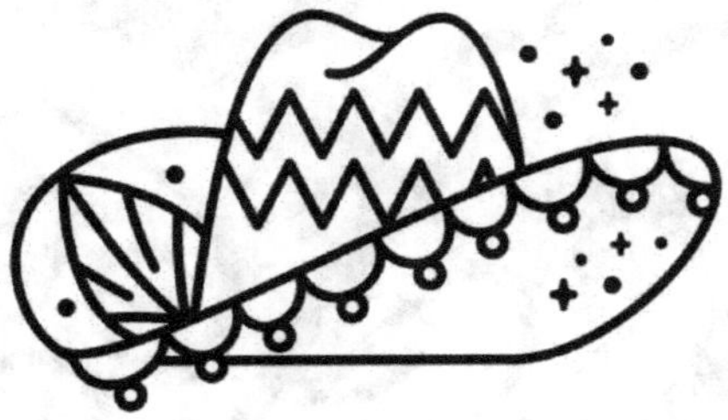

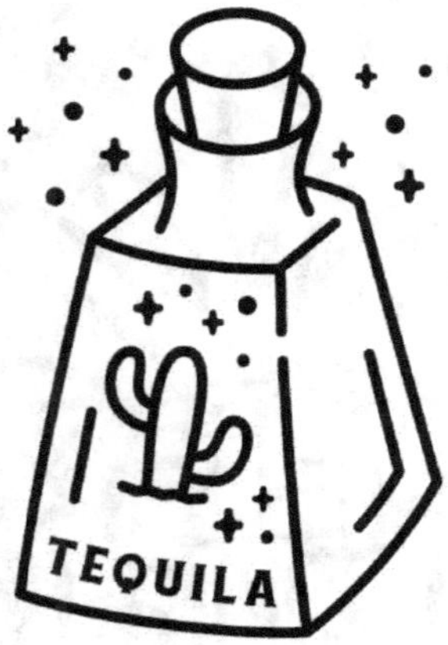
TEQUILA

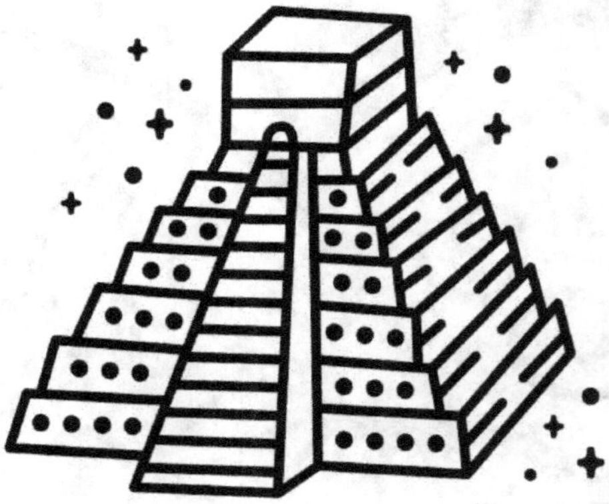

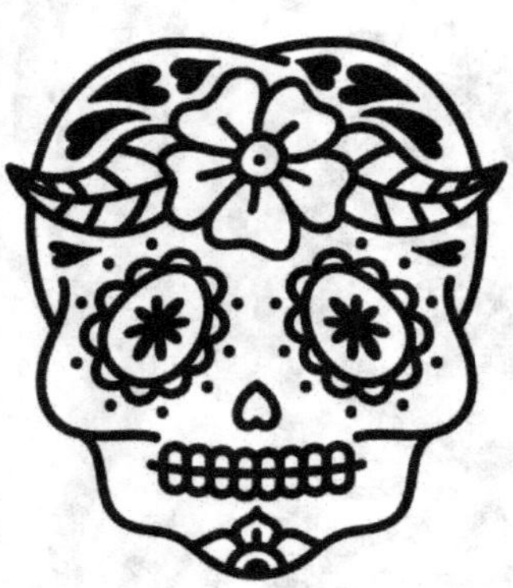

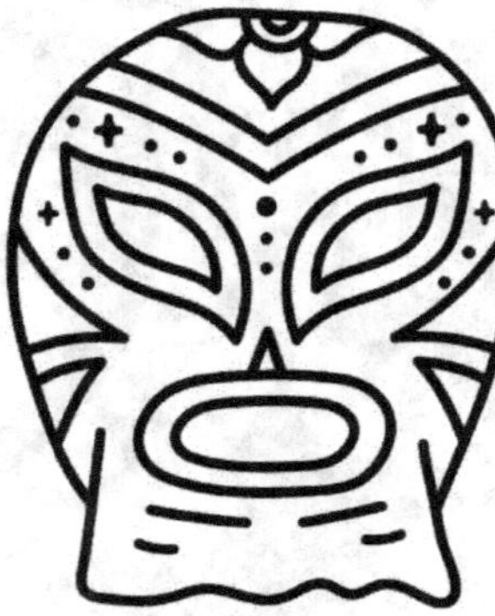

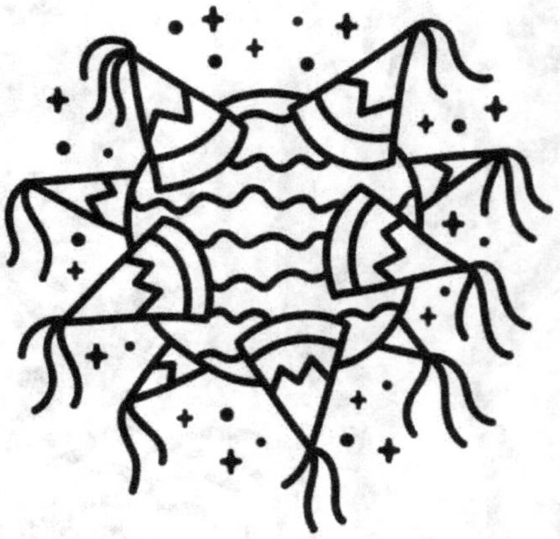

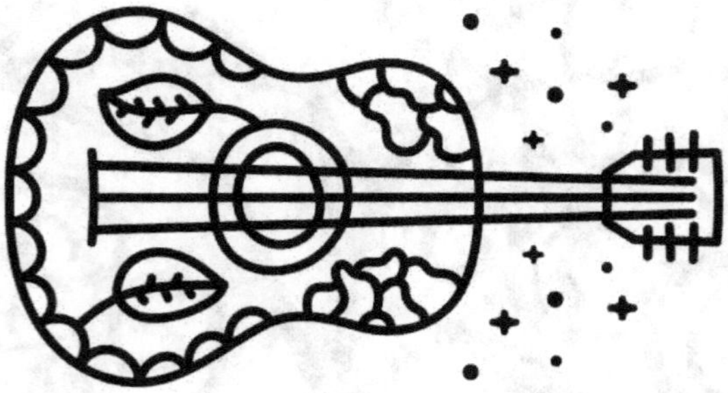

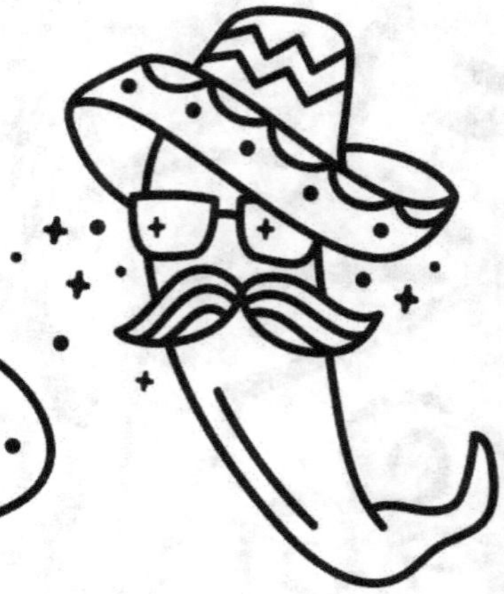

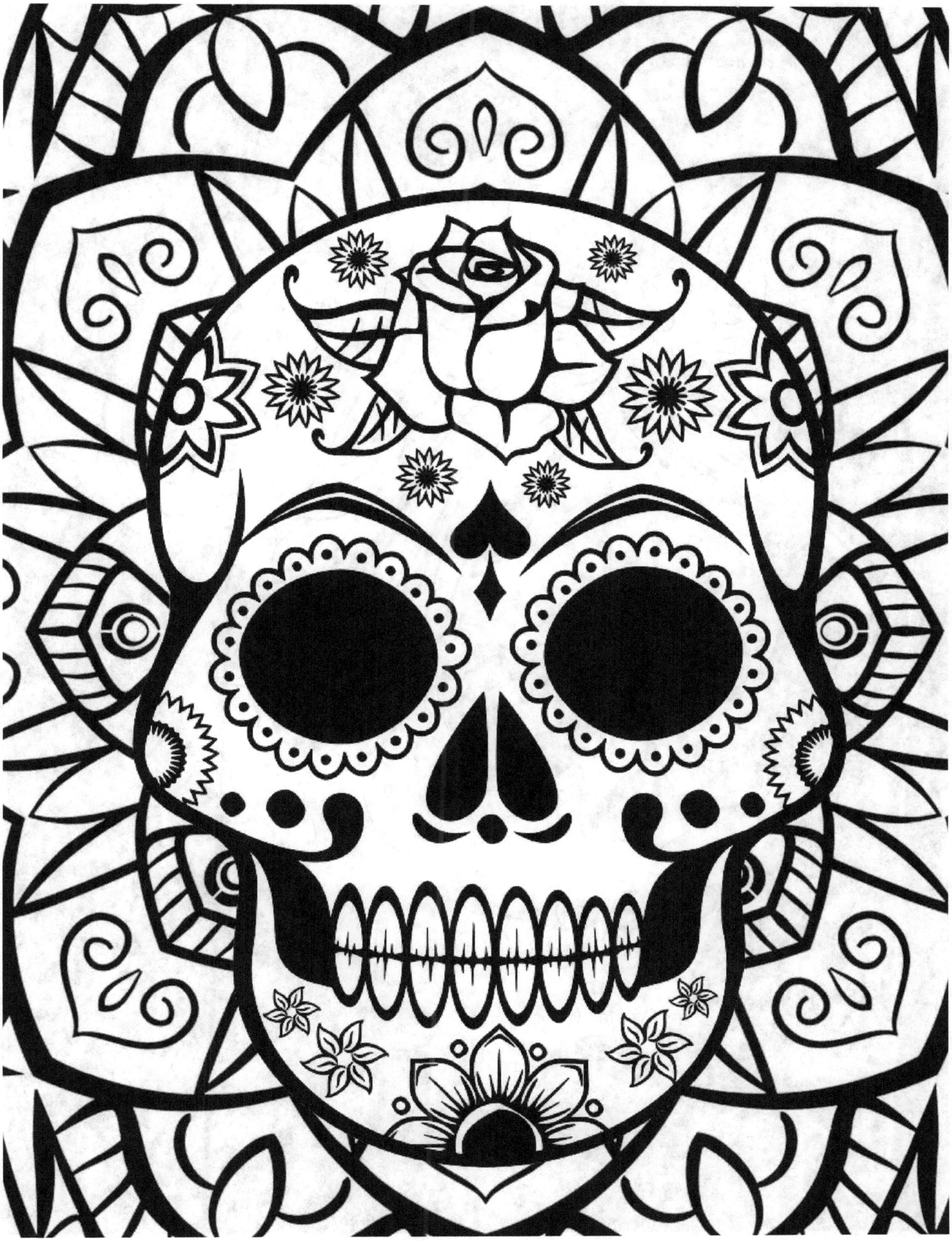

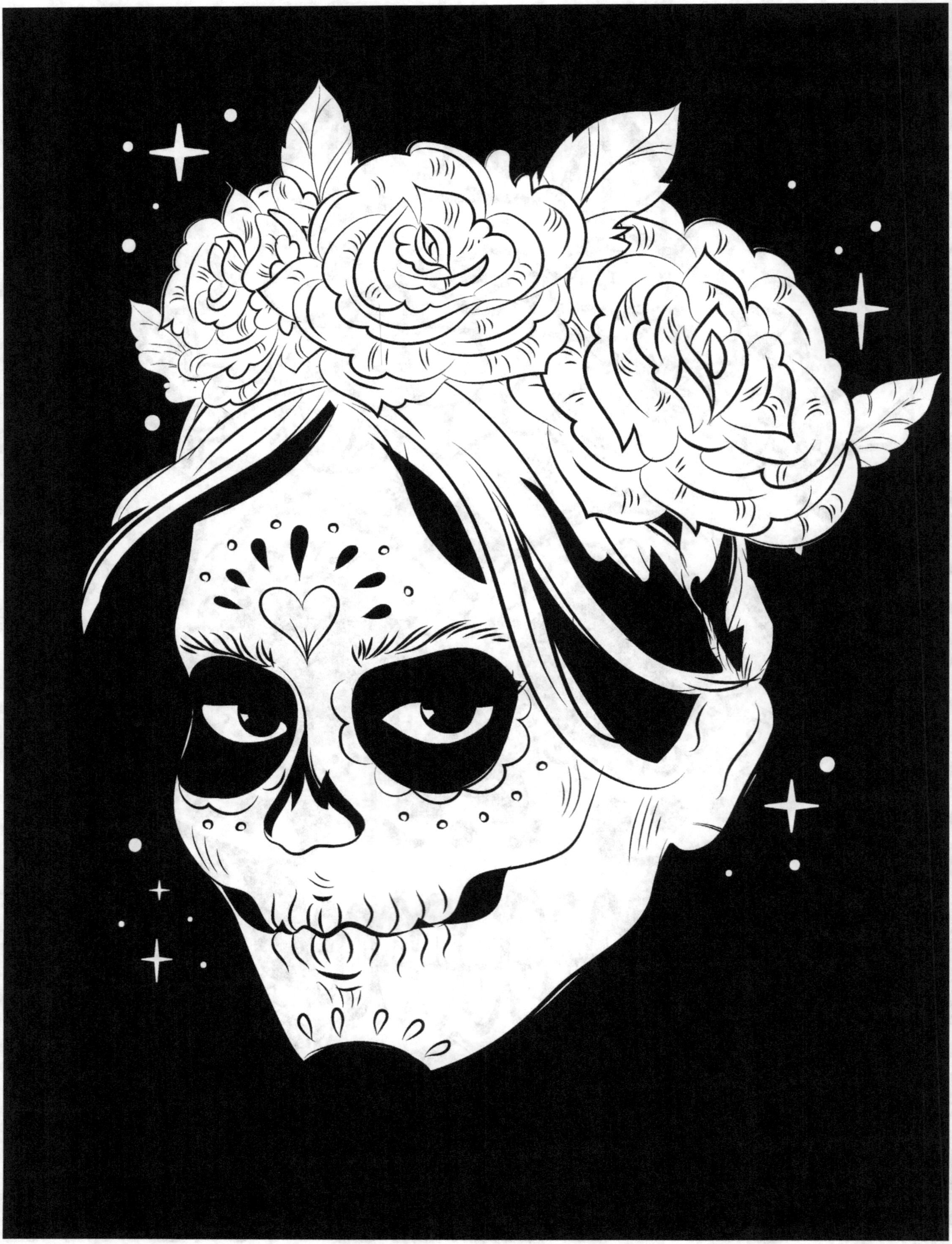

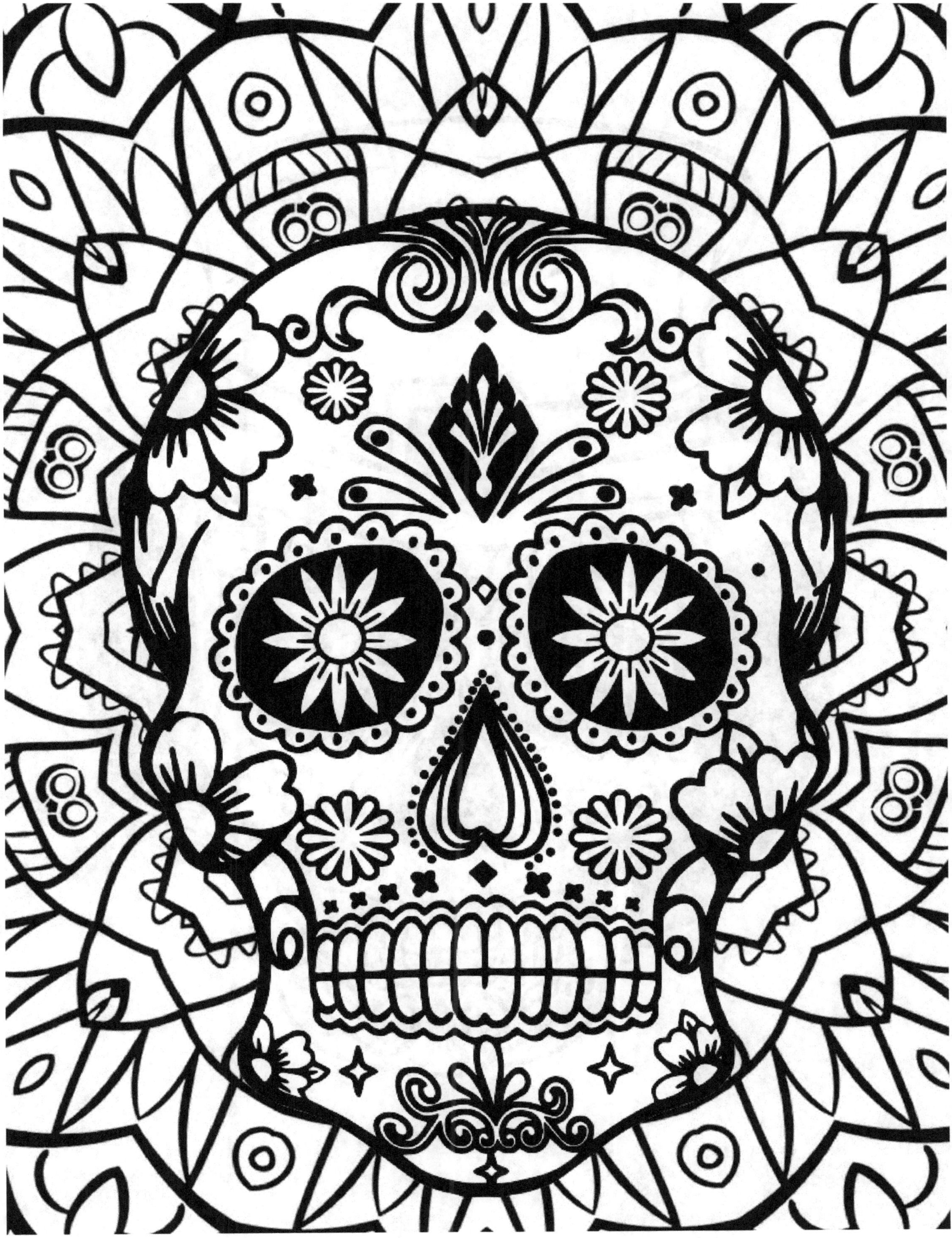

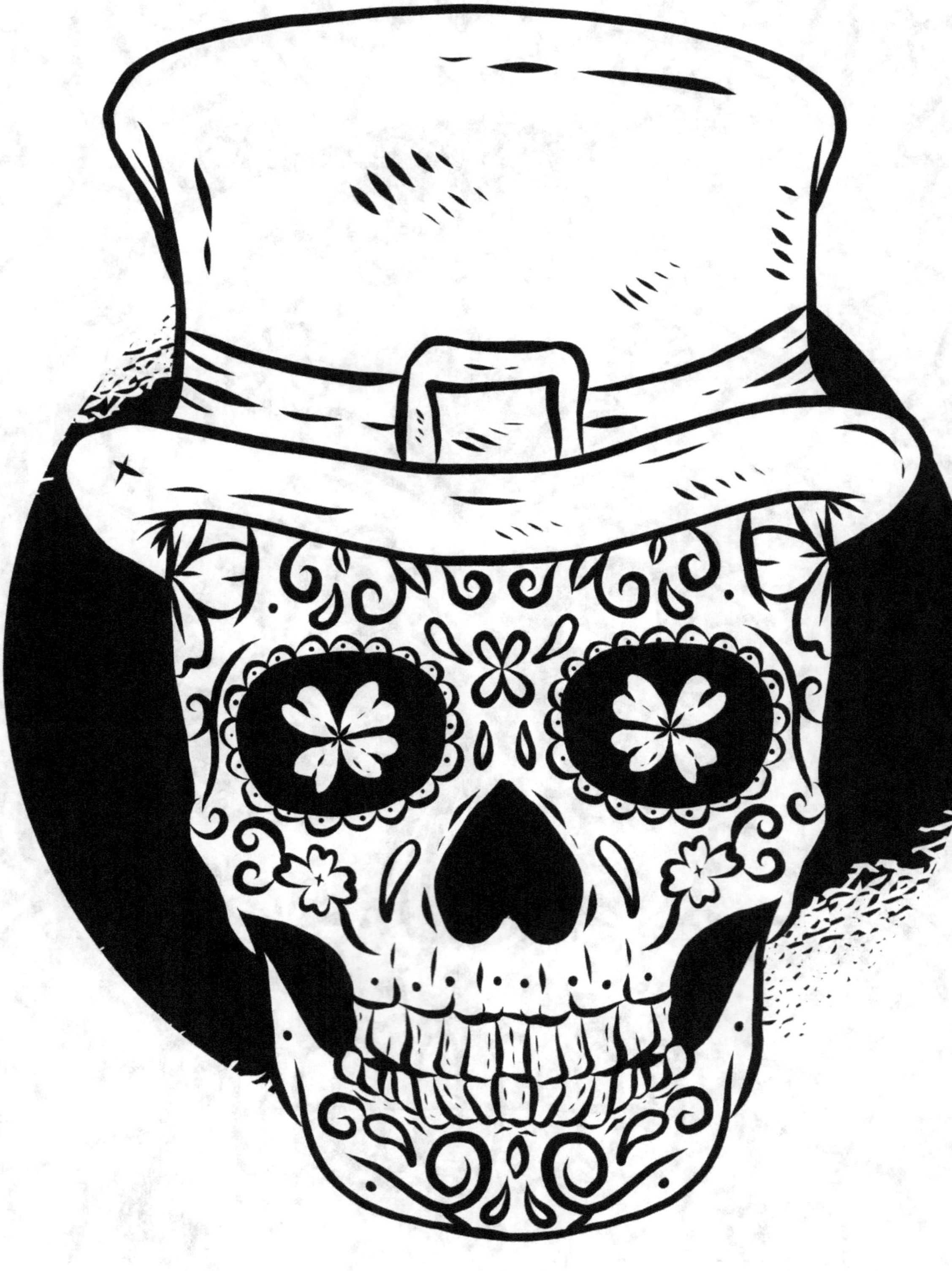

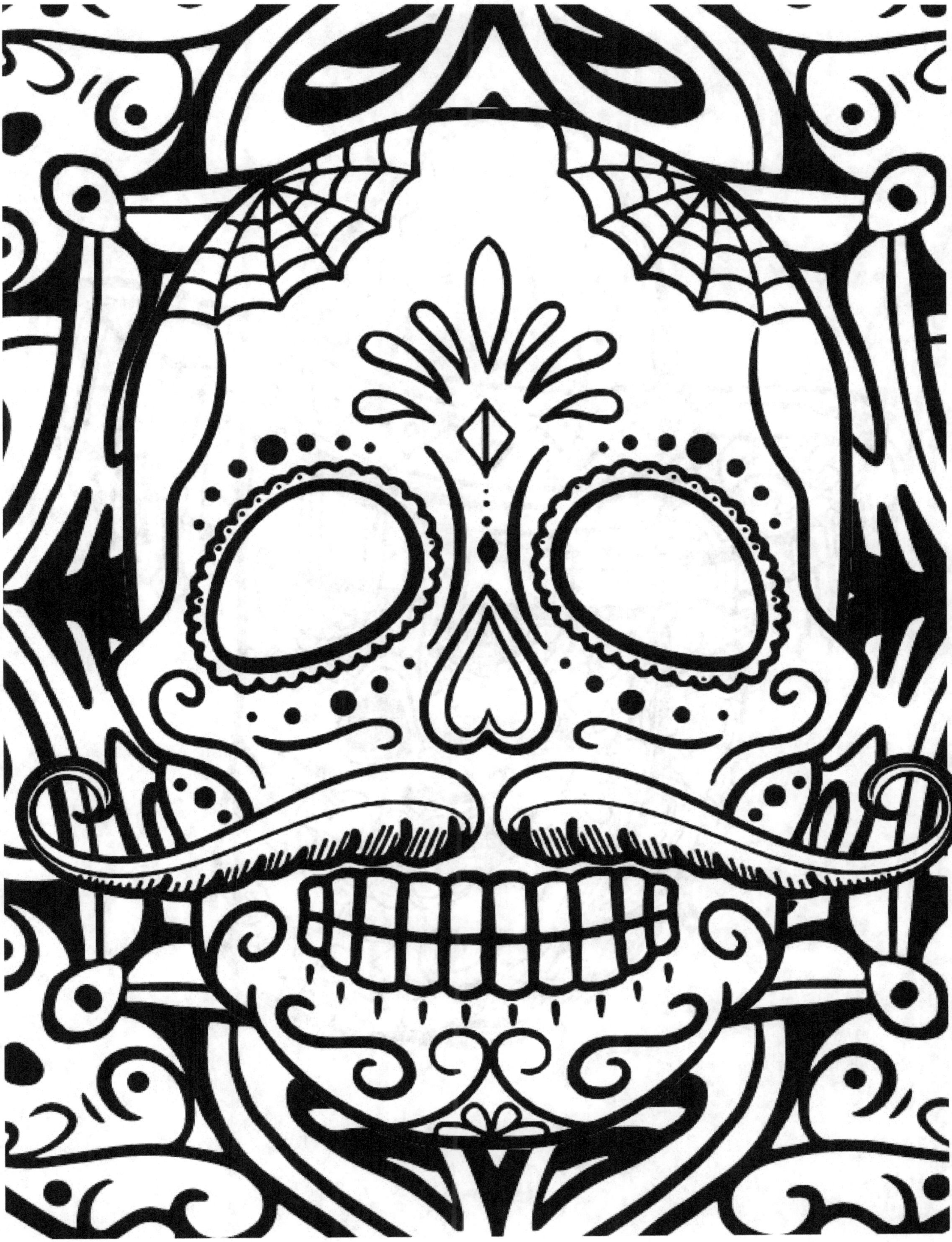

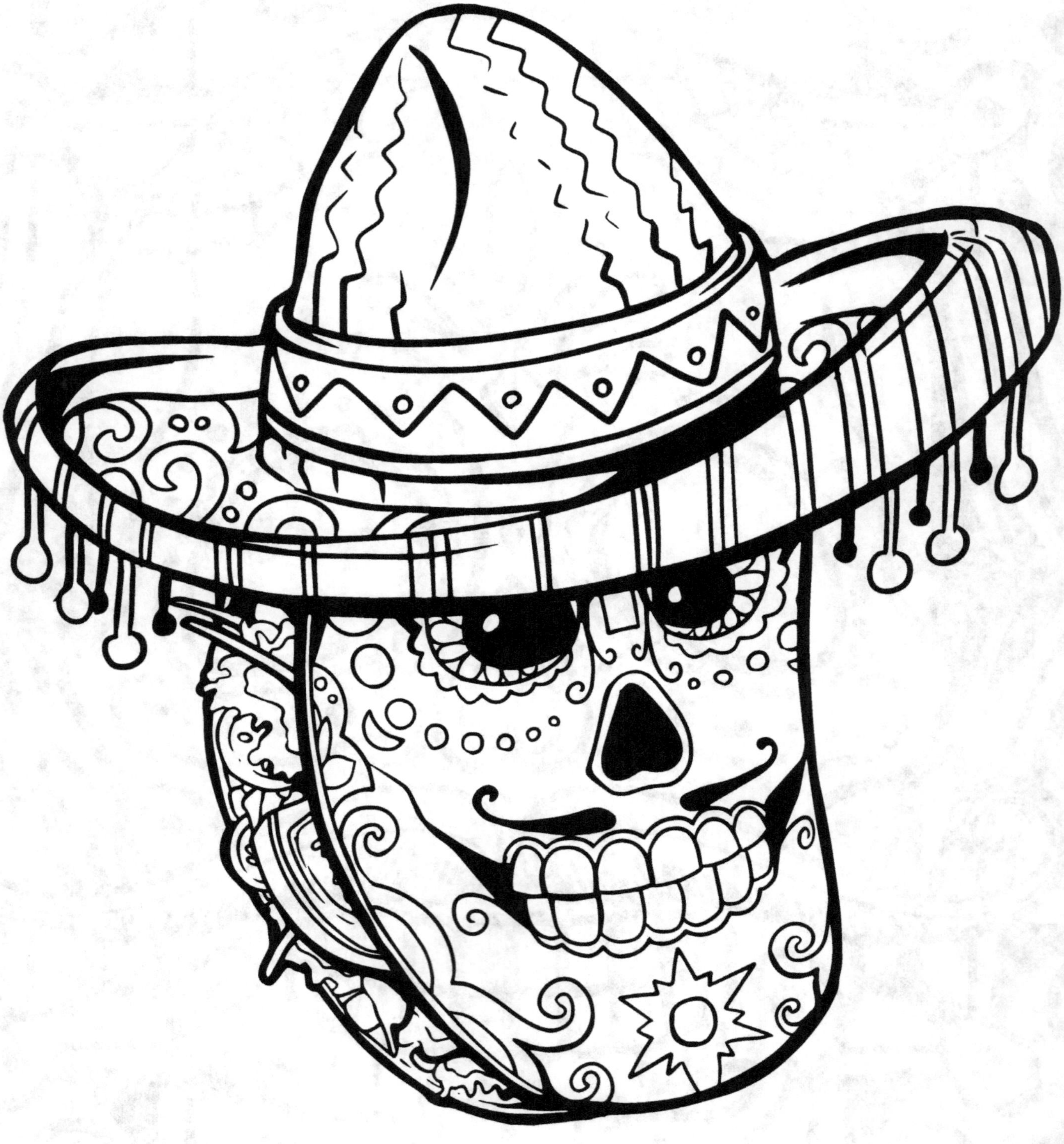

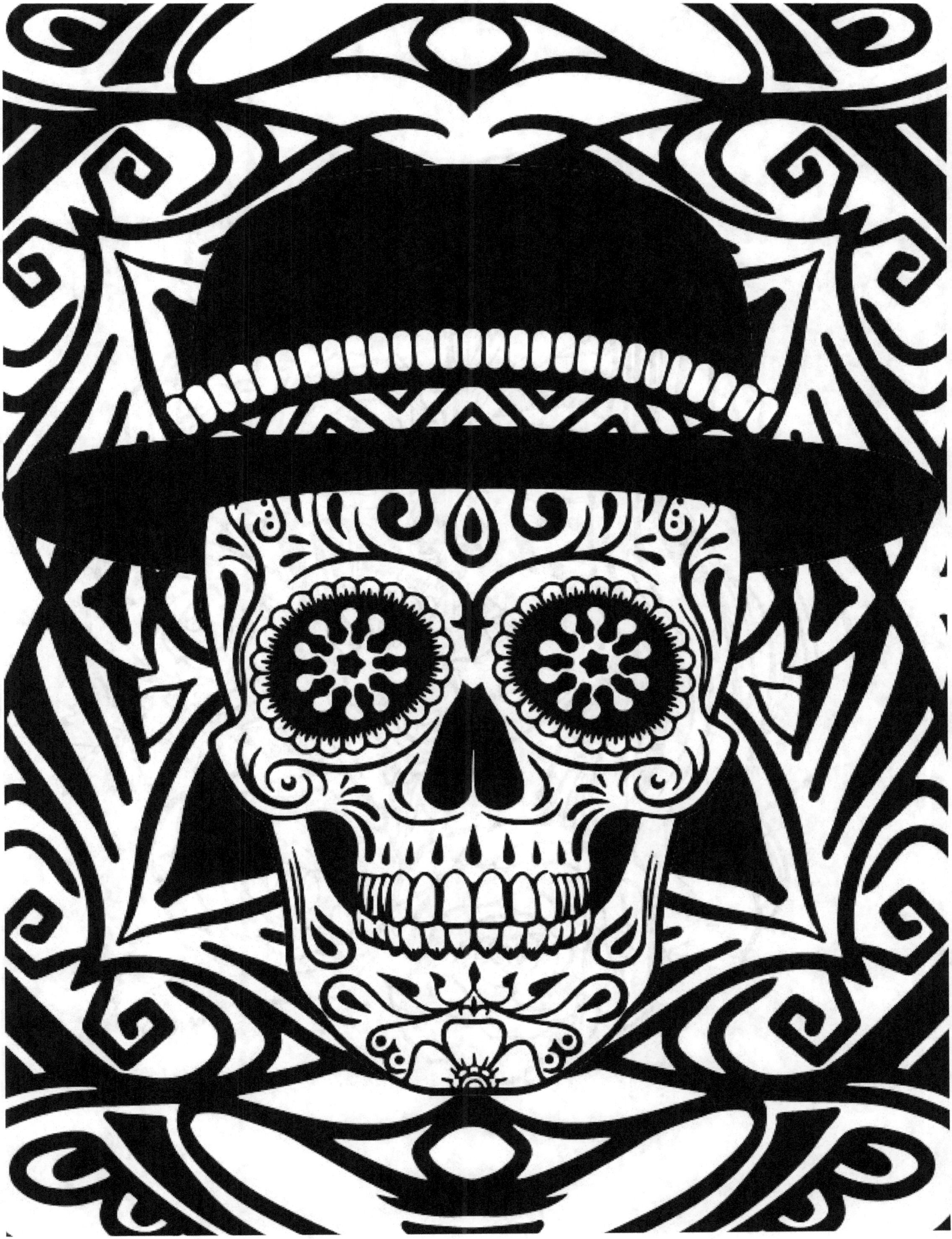

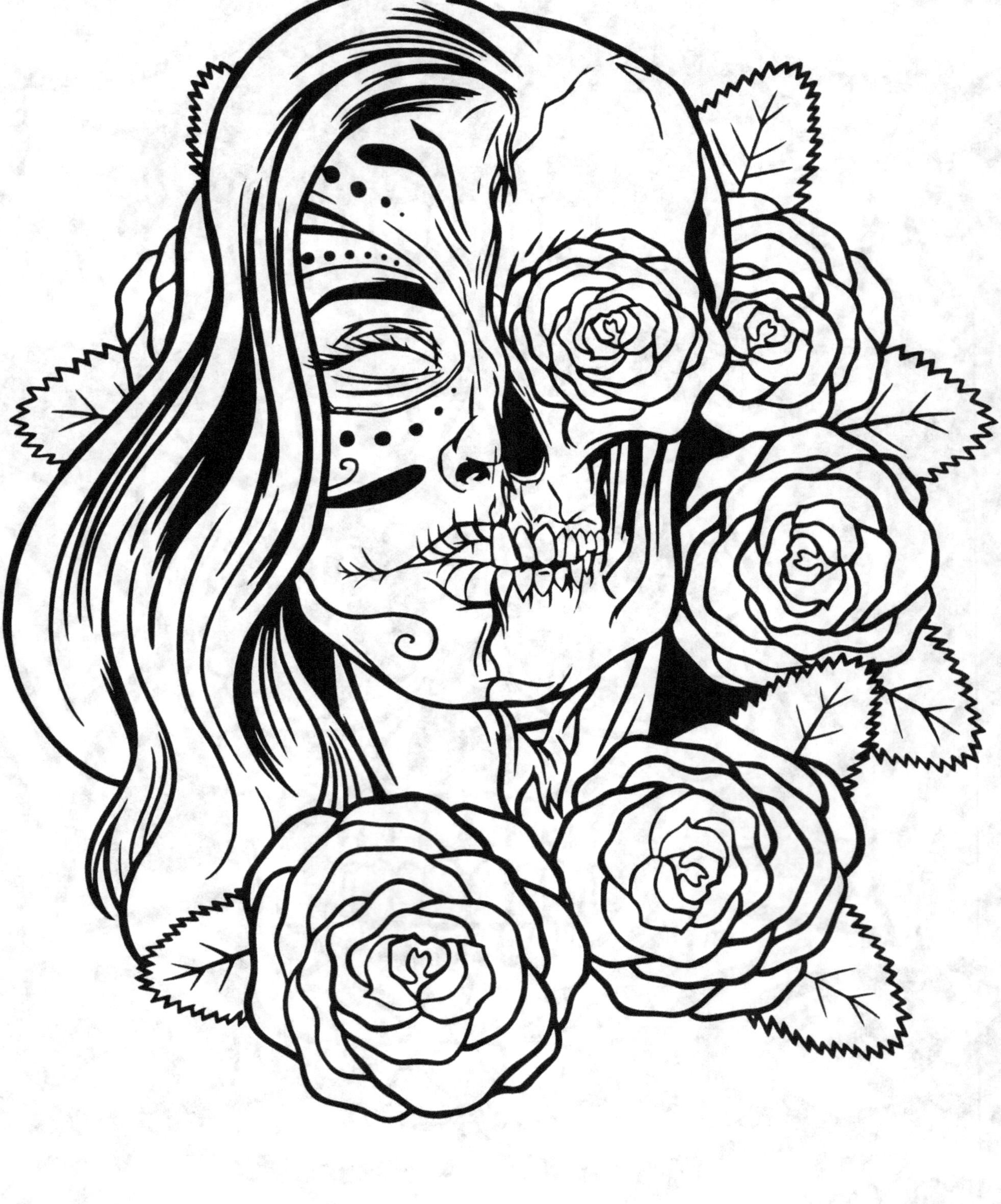

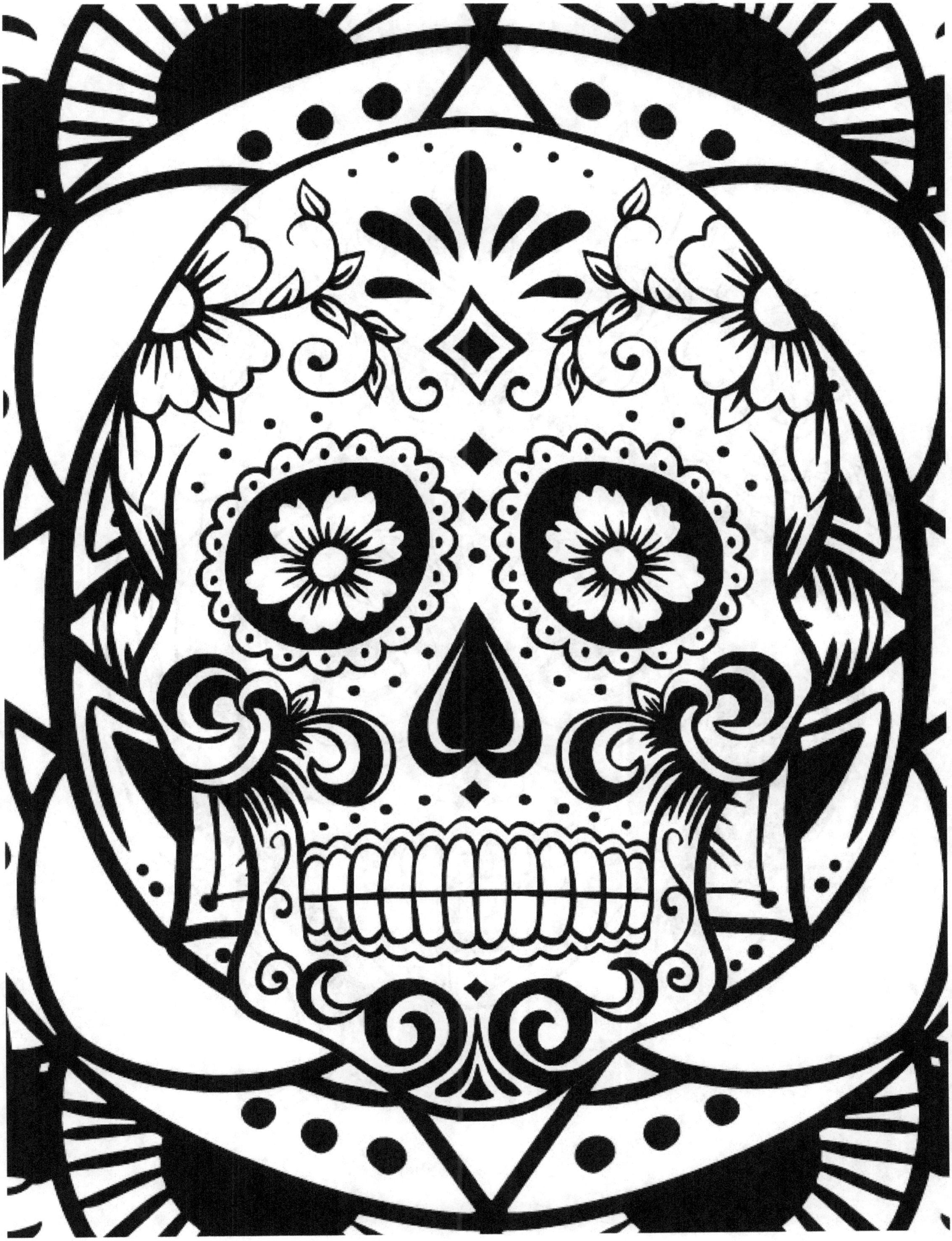

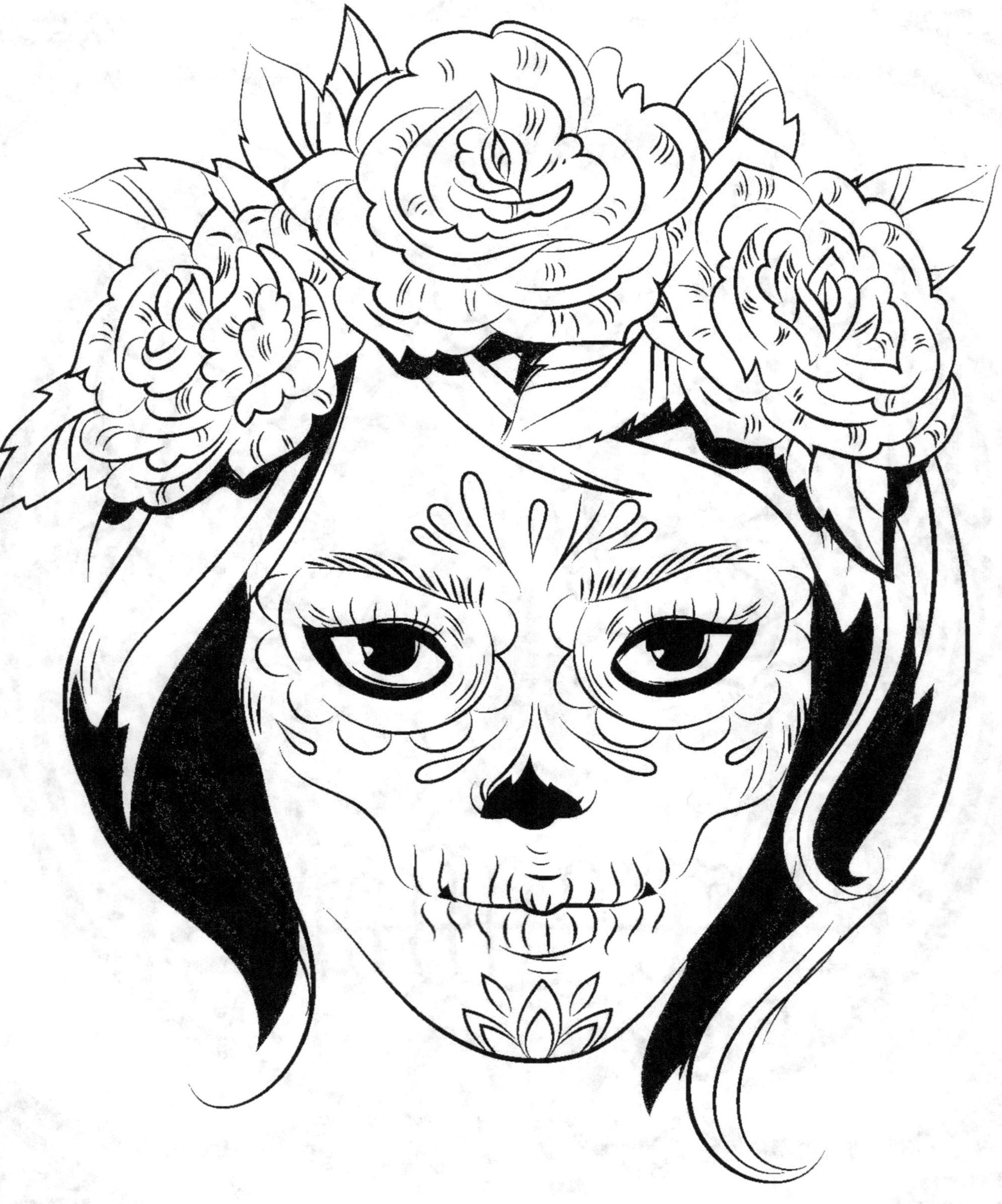

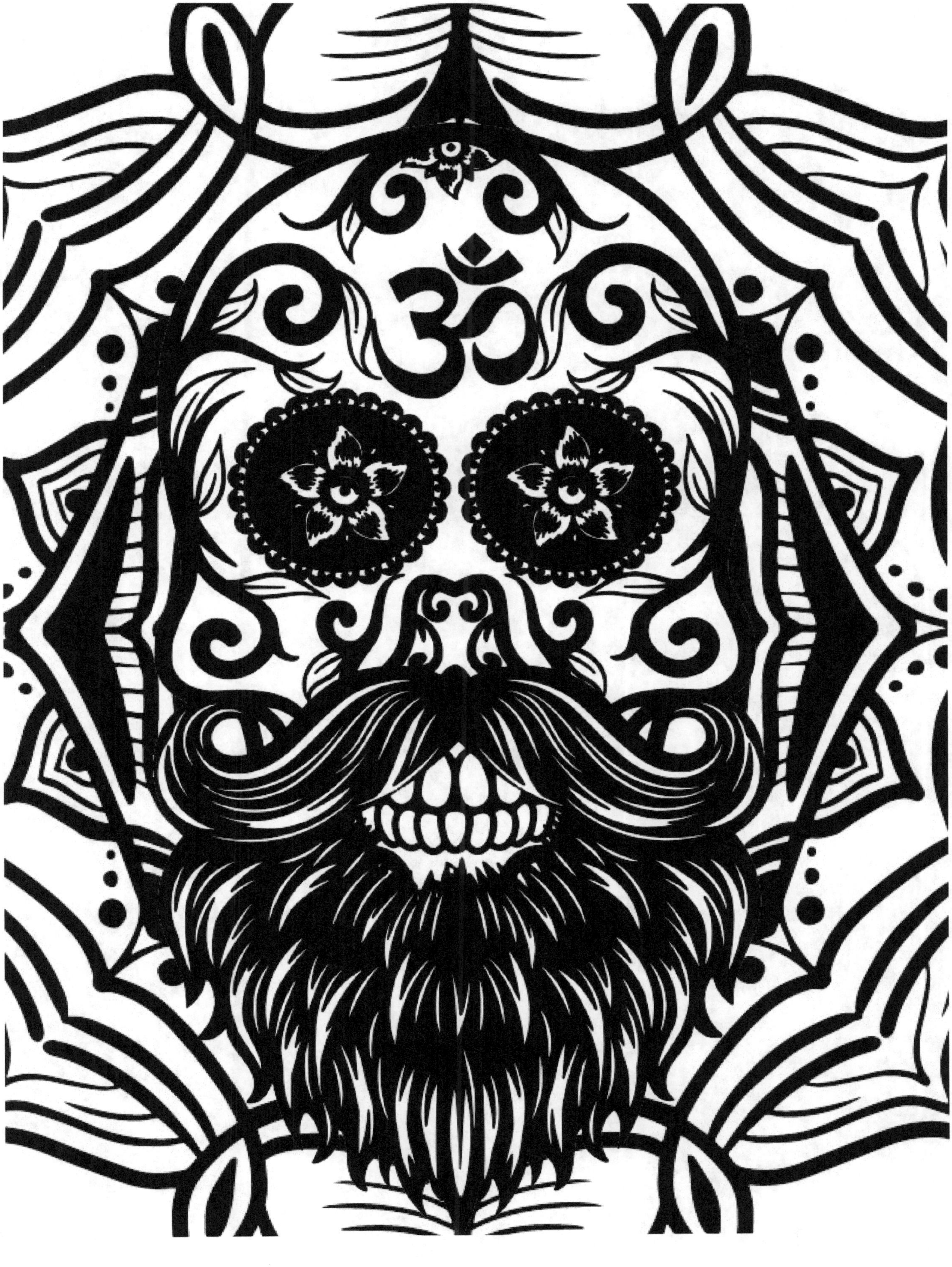

www.ingramcontent.com/pod-product-compliance
Lightning Source LLC
Chambersburg PA
CBHW080620220526
45466CB00010B/3407
9798556999961